T0144322

How to Use Your Healing Power

How to Use Your Healing Power

The Meaning of the Healings of Jesus

Joseph Murphy
Ph.D., D.D.

Published 2019 by Gildan Media LLC
aka G&D Media
www.GandDmedia.com

Design by Meghan Day Healey of Story Horse, LLC

Library of Congress Cataloging-in-Publication Data is available upon request

ISBN: 978-1-7225-0129-7

10   9   8   7   6   5   4   3   2   1

Contents

Contents

Introduction

This book is written in response to thousands of requests from students in many parts of the world. One of the largest classes I have ever given was at the Wilshire Ebell Theatre, Los Angeles, California, on the healing miracles of Jesus and what they mean to men everywhere. This book is an attempt to elaborate on the inner meaning of the recorded healings in the New Testament and to show the reader that he can apply the Healing Principle today in the same way that Jesus did about two thousand years ago.

The stories of mental and physical illnesses recorded in the Bible have reoccurred from time immemorial to the present moment. You may see the conditions and symptoms of diseases described in the Bible in almost any hospital in the country. It is true, of course, that the diseases described today have scientific names derived from medical terminology.

All over the world today men and women of various creeds are awakening to the tremendous therapeutic results following the application of mental and spiritual laws. In the fields of medicine, psychiatry, psychology, and other related fields, evidence is being adduced and articles written on the effect of destructive mental and emotional conflicts as the cause of all kinds of disease. This is prophetic of the termination of the power of the five senses, the reign of so-called *matter*, and the reestablishment of the reign of Divine Intelligence and of the Infinite Healing Presence behind all things.

The Bible is a psychological textbook which teaches us how to overcome all problems. It explains how we get into trouble; then teaches us how to get out of trouble. It teaches a science of life. A knowledge of the meaning of symbols, the science of the Hebrew alphabet, and the meaning of the various names in the Bible forms the key to all the stories in the Bible. You may find the meaning of the various names given in the bible in *Strong's Concordance* or *Young's Concordance*. There are many other reference books but the above two are generally used by all Bible students interested in the inner meaning of the Bible.

To fully understand what another speaks or writes, it is necessary to tune in with the writer, claiming and knowing that his ideas, thoughts, words, and feelings are reproduced in our mind. We do not really know who wrote the Gospels, and as I write or speak on these wonderful Bible stories, I say to my Deep Self in meditation, "What did I as the writer of these stories mean when I wrote them?" Then I get quiet and still, feeling the Living Intelligence within flowing through my conscious mind revealing to me everything I need to know. There is only one mind. A memory of everything that has ever transpired is within your subjective mind, and it is possible for you to tune in. In a state of intercommunion of mind with mind, it is possible to have transmitted to your mind all the thoughts, ideas, and feelings of another mind with which you are in tune or *en rapport*. This is possible without the ordinary channels of sensuous communication. There is but one mind common to all individual men.

The purpose of this book, so far as possible, is to divest and strip these stories of the Bible of all mystery so that it will be an open book for all mankind. The same Healing Presence which Moses, Elijah, Paul, and Jesus used is available to you now. Use it and go forward in the Light, moving from glory to glory *until the dawn appears, and the shadows flee away.*

1

Healing Of Mental Disorders

The following quotation is taken from the fourth chapter of Luke. It forms the sound basis for all healing, and tells all of us what we are here for.

The Spirit of the Lord is upon me, because he hath anointed me to preach the gospel to the poor; he hath sent me to heal the broken-hearted, to preach deliverance to the captives, and recovering of sight to the blind, to set at liberty them that are bruised. And he closed the book, and he gave it again to the minister, and sat down. And the eyes of all them that were in the synagogue were fastened on him. And he began to say unto them, This day is this scripture fulfilled in your ears. LUKE 4:18–21.

Here is one of the most remarkable and extraordinary statements in the whole Bible. *This day is this scripture fulfilled in your ears.* Not tomorrow or next week or next year, but NOW, this minute. *God is the Eternal Now.* Your good is this moment. Claim your health now, your peace now. The Healing Principle and the Peace of God are within you. Someone asked me in our class on "The Healing Miracles" if the healing stories in the Bible were true. The answer to the question is very simple. If the use of the Healing Principle is going on all the time and is applicable to all people all of the time everywhere, it is certainly truer, more interesting, and more fascinating than if it were an historic event of a certain date, a definite geographical location, and confined to just certain people.

In order to understand your Bible see it as a great psychological drama taking place in the consciousness of all people everywhere when they pray scientifically. Look upon the following dramatic episodes recorded in the Bible as stories about yourself and your friends awakening from darkness to the Light within. You can call Jesus in the Bible, as Robert Taylor of Cambridge, England, in 1829 did, *illumined reason.* Your concordance gives you many meanings for Jesus such as "God is savior," or "God is your solution, or salvation." In other words the names Joshua and Jesus are identical. The meaning is that your awareness or faith in the God-Wisdom can do all things. Look upon Jesus as yourself possessed of faith and confidence looking at the thoughts, beliefs, and opinions of your mind (your synagogue) rejecting all the false beliefs, theories, and ideas and announcing the presence of your ideal or the state desired. You do this in the present tense.

The Bible writer tells you that no matter what you are seeking, it exists now. Why wait for a healing? Why postpone it? Why say, "Some day I will have peace." The God of peace is within. The Power of the Almighty is within, and you will receive energy and strength. Love is here this moment, and you can experience the Divine Love welling up in your heart for all people. You can also attract your divine companion now. What you are seeking in the future is present now, right where you are. Your knowledge of the laws of your mind is your savior.

And they were astonished at his doctrine: for his word was with power. And in the synagogue there was a man, which had a spirit of an unclean devil, and cried out with a loud voice, Saying, Let us alone; what have we to do with thee, thou Jesus of Nazareth? art thou come to destroy us? I know thee who thou art; the Holy One of God. And Jesus rebuked him, saying, Hold thy peace, and come out of him. And when the devil had thrown him in the midst, he came out of him, and hurt him not. Luke 4:32–35. *Related passages,* Mark 1:23–27, 3:11, 7:25–30.

There was a belief in ancient times that when a man was insane he was possessed by demons or devils. This had its corollary in the belief that all psychotic or mentally deranged people were demon possessed. In Bible days exorcism in its varied forms became the regularly accepted form of therapy for the mentally disordered patients. Even today in some parts of America and even here in Los Angeles a student will say, "Oh, I think he or she is possessed by a demon." At one time people tried varying methods in order to drive demons out of the mind or body of the person. Today the psychiatrist, psychologist, and spiritual leader tries to bring about an adjustment of the personality and a cleansing of the mind of all negative thoughts and false beliefs. You are very familiar with the sudden and miraculous change often seen nowadays when a manic-depressive condition of an individual is cured by shock therapy.

Many years ago when a boy traveling on an ocean liner to India, I saw a raving maniac completely healed by an American woman who prayed aloud for him. He had a remarkable, instantaneous healing. Being curious, I asked her what she did. She replied, "I claimed that God's love and peace filled his mind." Today I understand much better what she meant. Her realization of the presence and power of God in the man was instantaneously resurrected in his mind, and a healing followed. Her faith made him whole. This is the whole story from a spiritual standpoint.

All *demons* or *devils* are negative states of mind that have been developed because the creative power of man has been used in an ignorant and destructive manner. The work of every man is to go into his own *synagogue* (mind) and through spiritual awareness cast out of his own mind the false theories, dogmas, beliefs, opinions, as well as all negative states such as resentment, ill will, hatred, jealousy, etc. These are the devils which bedevil us. Obsessions, dual personalities, and all other mental aberrations are the result of habitual negative thinking, crystallizing into definite states of mind such as complexes and other various poison pockets in the subconscious.

You are empowered to cast out demons by affirming your unity and oneness with the indwelling God; then you silently or audibly with feeling and faith speak the word of health, harmony, and peace. Pray with confidence like the woman on board the ship referred to previously by silently concentrating on the dissolving Power of God's Love upon the person. Thus the hold of evil thoughts will be broken.

The supposed devil cries out, *Let us alone, what have we to do with thee.* And he rebuked him saying, *Hold thy peace, come out of him.*

To rebuke means that you completely reject, once and for all, the power of any so-called negative or evil force. You do not admit for one moment that demons have any power, or that there are such entities.

He suffered not the demons to speak. MARK 1:34.

This means that you, who are illumined by the Light, will not, under any circumstances, permit negative race thoughts to dissuade you to turn away from the belief in One Supreme Power which is One and Indivisible. The method of healing used by Jesus here was the word of authority, . . . *for with authority and power he commandeth the unclean spirits, and they came out.* LUKE 4:36.

Your word is your awareness, your feeling, your conviction. Psychologically it is the union of the conscious and subconscious mind; *i.e.,* you have reached the point of agreement or complete mental acceptance of that which you affirm as true. The moment you accept it completely without reservations, the healing takes place in the person for whom you are praying. If you are praying for a mentally deranged person, follow the teachings of the Bible herein set forth.

Go boldly into your synagogue, which means the temple of your own mind; there gather your thoughts together rehearsing in your mind the Truths about God in the presence of your assembled thoughts and opinions; and therein feel the mental atmosphere of freedom and peace of mind for the sick person. Become Jesus (illumined mind) now; *i.e.*, you are full of faith and confidence as you enter the realm of your mind, giving no power to symptoms, or the nature of the mental blocks. Reject completely the verdict and opinions of those around you. Do this emphatically and with a sense of inner knowing. Know that you have the authority to speak the word; *i.e.*, to feel and know that your thought is authoritative inasmuch as it is the Infinite thinking through you.

Quimby, the great American healer, knew that when he thought of his patient he was in command of the other person's mind and body; then he contemplated his divine perfection. He duplicated many of the miracles recorded in the Bible. Quimby's inner conviction that what was true of God was true of his patient was the word that he sent. *He sent his word and healed them.*

There are many evil spirits (negative emotions) such as hatred, resentment, revenge, jealousy, etc. It could be said that a man with intense hatred is obsessed by an evil spirit. Your mood or emotion is the spirit operating at the human level. The law governing your subjective mind is that it is amenable to suggestion. In ancient times, the idea was current that any one was liable at any time to be taken possession of by a devil. Many persons who easily entered the subjective condition through fear found themselves possessed by devils, *i.e.*, the power of their own fearful thoughts.

In ancient times and even today in some parts of the world the profession of exorcism was and is a very profitable one. The general belief was that the demons were afraid of holy water, the Bible, and of hearing the name of God pronounced. Accordingly it came to pass that, upon the verbal command of the exorcist the so-called devil would often incontinently fly, leaving the patient free. Sometimes the patient would go into convulsions on hearing the magic name pronounced, and more exorcists were then employed. You can see that the whole procedure is one of belief, and according to the belief of the exorcist is it done unto him.

Doctors and scientists are conducting experiments in hypnosis; they know, for example, that they can cause a subject under hypnosis to act like an insane person by suggestion. For instance, in a trance state a man can be told he will jump with one foot in the air when he sees a dog, and he will jump. If given a posthypnotic suggestion, he will repeat the performance after being awakened. This is a compulsion. He can be told he is possessed by a bad spirit or devil, and his subconscious mind which acts upon suggestion, faithfully reproduces the role of a devil with the same extraordinary acumen that it would personate any other character suggested. The subconscious mind which is all things to all men will exhibit as many different kinds and degrees of deviltry as there are devils embraced in the suggestion. Experimentally any type of insanity can be brought about by appropriate suggestions given to subjects in the trance state. In experiments when the suggestion is relieved, the subject being instructed that it was only a suggestion, the mental aberrations disappear. The schizophrenic, psychotic, depressive type, manic type of insanities can be demonstrated by suggestion. It is easy to see where the so-called devils come from.

The ceremony of exorcism which is even today in use by certain organizations constitutes a most powerful suggestive command to the subjective mind; according to the faith of the operator the desired result is achieved. The fact that the trouble is susceptible of cure by a ritual or ceremony points clearly to its mental origin, precluding the possibility of its being attributable to extra mundane causes or external entities.

Many people come to see me and write me saying that they hear voices all the time, and what terrible things these voices are saying. They believe they are possessed by evil spirits. I tell them that I hear voices also. Clairaudience is a faculty of the human mind. It is that faculty of intelligence within you which enables your objective mind to receive communications from your own subjective mind, or from another by means of spoken words.

A few weeks ago I clearly heard an answer to a question which had perplexed me for some time. I heard the words clearly. These words did not come from some discarnate entity but they came from my own subjective self which is one with Boundless Wisdom and Infinite Intelligence. When you receive ideas from the subjective, or when the answer comes, it is necessarily by such means as can be understood by you, *i.e.*, by means which appeal to your senses. There are many people who hear clairaudiently; some attribute it to imagination, others regard it as a subjective hallucination. Some attribute this phenomenon of hearing words from the subjective mind to spirits of the departed; needless to say, the same law of suggestion applies and governs the character of their clairaudient manifestation.

The subconscious mind will assume the characters suggested by the conscious mind. If, for example, you believe it is a guardian angel speaking to you, or the voice of a disembodied spirit, the subconscious will follow the suggestion given, and all further communication will be conducted on the basis assumed by you. Your subconscious will assume the character of an angel or devil according to the suggestion given.

Some months ago a young man from a local university came to see me with the complaint that he was constantly hearing spirit-voices, that they made him do nasty things, and that they would not let him alone, neither would they permit him to read the Bible or other spiritual books. He was convinced that he was talking to supernatural beings. This young man was clairaudient, and not knowing that all people possess this faculty, he began to think it was due to evil spirits. His superstitious beliefs caused him to ascribe it to departed spirits. Through constant worry he became a monomaniac on the subject. His subconscious mind dominated and controlled by an all-potent but false suggestion, gradually took over control and mastery of his objective faculties, and his reason abdicated its throne. He was what you would call mentally unbalanced, as all men are who allow their false beliefs to obtain the ascendancy.

We must not place gangsters, assassins, and murderers in charge of our mind. Place Wisdom and Divine Love in charge of your mind. Let faith in God, and all things good take charge of your mind. The subjective or subconscious mind within each of us is of tremendous importance and significance, but it can be influenced negatively and positively. Be sure that you influence it only positively, constructively, and harmoniously. The subconscious possesses transcendent powers, but it is at the same time amenable to good and bad suggestions. The explanations which I gave him made a profound impression on him.

I gave him the following written prayer which he was to repeat for ten or fifteen minutes three or four times a day: "God's Love, Truth, and Wisdom flood my mind and heart. I love the Truth, I hear the Truth, and I know the Truth. God's River of Peace floods my mind, and I give thanks for my freedom."

He repeated the above prayer slowly, quietly, reverently, and with deep feeling, particularly prior to sleep. By identifying with harmony and peace, he brought about a rearrangement of the thought patterns and imagery of his mind, and a healing followed. He knew that what was true of God was true of himself. He brought about a conviction by repetition, faith, and expectancy.

My prayer for him night and morning was as follows: "John is thinking rightly. He is reflecting Divine Wisdom and Divine Intelligence in all ways. His mind is the perfect mind of God, unchanging and eternal. He hears the Voice of God which is the Voice of Peace and Love. He understands the Truth, he knows the Truth, and he loves the Truth. God's River of Peace floods his mind. His mind is full of God's Wisdom and Understanding. Whatever is vexing him now is leaving him, and I pronounce him free and at peace."

I meditated on these words of Truth night and morning, getting the "feel" of peace and harmony; at the end of a week this young man was completely free. I fasted from the poisoned feast of sense evidence and fear-symptoms. I had to cure myself of the belief in a diseased state, and outer results necessarily followed. I think my explanation was a great help to this young man. The ill state is conditioned in us as long as we see that state of illness portrayed. Our failure is due to absence of faith in the disciples (our mental faculties). We must contemplate the Infinite Perfection within us, and keep on doing so, until the day breaks and the shadows flee away.

He suffered not the demons to speak.

2

How Your Mind Heals the Sick

And he arose out of the synagogue, and entered into Simon's house. And Simon's wife's mother was taken with a great fever; and they besought him for her. And he stood over her, and rebuked the fever; and it left her: and immediately she arose and ministered unto them. LUKE 4:38–39. *Related passage,* MATT. 8:14–15.

Some time ago, a woman told me her child had a very high fever and was not expected to live. The doctor had prescribed small doses of aspirin, and had administered an antibiotic preparation. The mother was involved in a contemplated divorce action and was terribly agitated and emotionally disturbed. This disturbed feeling was communicated subconsciously to the child, and naturally the child got ill.

Children are at the mercy of their parents and are controlled by the dominant mental atmosphere of those around them. They have not yet reached the age of reason where they can take control of their own thoughts, emotions, and reactions to life. This mother, at my suggestion, decided to get quiet and still by reading the *Twenty-third Psalm,* praying for guidance, also praying for the peace and harmony of her husband, and pouring out love upon him instead of resentment and rage. The fever of the child was the suppressed anger and rage of the mother which was felt by the child and expressed as a high fever, or a state of excitation of the mind.

Having quieted her own mind, she began to pray for the child in this manner: "Spirit which is God is the life of my child. Spirit has no temperature; it is never sick or feverish. The peace of God floods my child's mind and body. The Harmony, Health, Love, and Perfection of God are made manifest in my child's mind and body now. She is relaxed and at ease, poised, serene, and calm. I am now stirring up the gift of God within her, and all is well."

She repeated the above prayer slowly, quietly, and lovingly for about ten minutes. She noticed a remarkable change in the child, who awakened, and asked for a doll and for something to eat. The temperature became normal. What happened? The fever left the child because the mother was no longer feverish or agitated in her mind. Her mood of peace, harmony, and love was instantaneously felt by the child, and a corresponding reaction was produced in the child. She took her child by the hand, biblically speaking.

The *hand* means the Power of God. With the hand you fashion, mold, shape, and direct. It is symbolic of the Creative Power or Intelligence in all of us. She lifted her child by the hand in the sense that she lifted up the idea of health, harmony, and peace in her mind to the point of acceptance, and the Power of the Almighty responded accordingly. It is the nature of the Deeper Mind to respond to the nature of your thought. When the mother focused her attention on the idea of perfect health for her child, the Power of the Almighty flowed through her focal point of attention, and a healing followed.

When the Bible speaks of *entering into Simon's house,* it refers to what you are hearing. The word *Simon* means to hear, and *Simon's wife's mother* means the emotional state which follows what you have been hearing or giving attention to. If disturbed by some news, or if you become unduly excited, you must rise up in your *synagogue* (mind); i.e., you should contemplate the Inner Presence as saturating every atom of your being. Then a wave of inner peace will follow, and all will be well. You rebuke the fever or sick state by contemplating the Omnipresence of God. This is Divine Science in action.

Great peace have they who love thy law and nothing shall offend them.

And it came to pass, when he was in a certain city, behold a man full of leprosy: who seeing Jesus fell on his face, and besought him, saying, Lord, if thou wilt, thou canst make me clean. And he put forth his hand, and touched him, saying, I will: be thou clean. And immediately the leprosy departed from him. And he charged him to tell no man: but go, and shew thyself to the priest, and offer for thy cleansing, according as Moses commanded, for a testimony unto them. LUKE 5:12–14. *Related passages,* MARK 1:40–44. MATT. 8:2–4.

A *leper,* biblically speaking, is a person who through erroneous thoughts has separated himself from the real Source of life. It means a man who is governed by the five senses, and is psychologically and spiritually separated from his Divine Center. A leprous or impure condition is the result of being governed by the five senses with its fears, superstitions, and erroneous thoughts.

He put forth his hand, and touched him, saying, I will: be thou clean. You have seen men lay hands on people, and pray over them, and a healing followed; this has occurred from time immemorial. Sometimes people refer to the man who practices the laying on of hands as a "natural born healer." Of course, we are all "natural born healers" for the simple reason that the Healing Presence of God is within all men. All of us can contact It with our thoughts. It responds to all. The Healing Principle is in the dog, the cat, the tree, and the bird. It is Omnipresent and is the Life of all things.

There are different degrees of faith. There is the man who, through faith, heals his ulcers, and another who heals a deep-seated, so-called incurable malignancy. It is as easy for the Healing Presence to heal a tubercular lung as a cut in the finger. There is no great or small in the God that made us all; there is no big or little, nor hard or easy. Omnipotence is within all men. The prayers of the man who lays his hand on another appeals to the cooperation of the unconscious; a response takes place, and *according to your faith* (feeling) *is it done unto you*. This is the time-honored procedure of healing.

And he charged him to tell no man. It is a wise procedure to refrain from going around telling everyone you had a spiritual healing. Many of your friends will pass derogatory and skeptical remarks which might undermine your faith, causing you to doubt and hence undo the benefits you received from the prayers of the healer and your own mental acceptance.

Shew thyself to the priest. When you pray, you are the *priest* offering up the *sacrifice.** Your feeling, mood, or attitude of receptivity is the connecting link between the Invisible and the visible. Your desire is your *offering;* you cleanse yourself by forgiving everyone, by sincerely wishing for all those who may have seemed to hurt you all of God's blessings such as peace, love, joy, and happiness. Having cleansed your mind of all impurities (negative imagery and destructive thoughts), you offer your gift (desire) to God by galvanizing yourself into the feeling of being one with your ideal. Become engrossed and absorbed in the joy of having heard the good news, or the joy of the answered prayer; this consumes the old state and gives birth to the new.

If you want a healing of your body, withdraw mentally from symptoms and evidence of senses and begin to think of God's Healing Presence within you. The five outward senses are now turned inward and focused on health and harmony. All your attention is on your health and peace of mind. The Almighty Creative Power flows through the focal point of attention. You feel the response of the Spirit flowing through you. The Healing Presence touches every atom of your being and you are spiritually enriched. Dwelling in conscious communion with the Divine, man often-

---

* See *Prayer Is the Answer.*

times becomes intoxicated with the Spirit. A state of exhilaration of the whole being takes place. This spiritual awakening builds up the entire man, makes him new, so that each day adds a new joy. As we continue to pray scientifically, we are lifted up so that an outpouring of Spirit takes place, and our whole being is revivified and recharged.

Dr. Alexis Carrel, in *Man The Unknown*, points out the marvelous effects produced by prayer. He cites a case of a cancerous sore which shriveled to a scar in front of his eyes. He recounts seeing wound-lesions heal in a few seconds, and pathological symptoms disappear in a few hours. Extreme activation of the processes of organic repair had set in. These healings of tumors, burns, etc., were due to nothing more than the release of the Healing Power within each one. God or Infinite Intelligence is the only Healer, the only Presence, the only Power. When we call on this Presence within, giving It supreme recognition, claiming that the Healing Power saturates our mind and body, we receive a corresponding flood of the Healing Power which permeates every atom of our body, cicatrizing wounds and making us whole. Our body begins to function harmoniously; its atomic and molecular formation once more is transformed into the way it is in the Divine Center within us; then we know the truth of the saying, *yet in my flesh shall I see God.*

When the Bible says, *offer for thy cleansing, according as Moses commanded*, you are to look at the word *Moses*, as Troward points out, as the Law—the way your deeper mind works. As you exalt your thought-patterns claiming and affirming your good, your deeper mind (the Law) automatically responds to the new mental pattern and mental imagery and a healing follows. The Law holds no grudges, no more so than the law of electricity. All you do is conform to the principle of electricity and results follow. You may have misused the principle for making water for fifty years; the moment you follow the correct procedure, you will get water.

And, behold, men brought in a bed a man which was taken with a palsy: and they sought means to bring him in, and to lay him before him. And when they could not find by what way they might bring him in because of the multitude, they went upon the housetop, and let him down through the tiling with his couch into the midst before Jesus. And when he saw their faith, he said unto him, Man, thy sins are forgiven thee. LUKE 5:18–20. *Related passage,* MARK 2:3–5.

I say unto thee, Arise, and take up thy couch, and go into thine house. LUKE 5:24.

I remember a case of palsy and tremors being treated some years ago. The man's legs would become locked so that inability to move was experienced.

Panic would ensue, and the man would be frozen to the spot even in the middle of a busy street. This condition of constant fear, panic, and foreboding was wearing him down. The following procedure was adopted. The first step was to get him out of nature's way. After *agreeing quickly with thy adversary* he was told he must not continue in a state of quarrel, fear, and panic as to why he was beset with such a physical condition, causes which brought it about, etc. He admitted to himself that the condition was present and quite a problem, but that he didn't have to have it. He said to himself, "I am going to deny the worst and return to the Rock from whence I came."

He turned to the God-Presence within which created him and knew what to do. This Healing Presence is Omnipresent, Omniscient, and Omnipotent. He aligned himself with the Infinite, realizing that the Healing Presence was saturating every atom of his being and flowing through him as harmony, health, peace, wholeness, and perfection. As he gradually filled his mind with these Eternal Verities, he became reconditioned to health and harmony. As he changed his mind, he changed his body, for the body is a shadow of the mind.

The Bible story says *men brought in a bed a man which was taken with a palsy.* The *bed* in which a man lies is his own mind. He lies down there with fear, doubt, condemnation, guilt, and superstition. These thoughts paralyze the mind and body.

In *Mark* 2:1–12 where we have a slightly different version of the same story, it says the man was *borne of four*. The numeral *four* represents the manifested world, the objective manifestation of subjective states of consciousness. *Four* means termination, the end result, the completion of a cycle of consciousness, negative or positive.

We are told that Jesus (awareness of the Power of God) healed him by *forgiving his sins. To sin* is to miss the mark, the goal of health, of happiness, of peace. We forgive ourselves by identifying mentally and emotionally with our ideal and continuing to do so until it jells within us as a conviction or subjective embodiment. We are, of course, sinning also when we think negatively or when we resent, hate, condemn, or fear another person. If we think there is some power to challenge the One Power (God), we are also sinning because we are cohabiting mentally with evil, thereby attracting all manner of calamity, trouble, and loss. We sin when we deviate or turn away from our announced goal or aim in life which should always be peace, harmony, wisdom, and perfect health. To indulge in morbid imagery and destructive thoughts, we mar our happiness and miss the target of a full and happy life.

Jesus forgave the paralytic by saying, *Arise, and take up thy couch*, which means that Truth or God never judges or condemns. The Absolute does not judge—all judgment is given to the son. All men are sons of the Infinite. Your mind is the son or offspring of the Spirit; with that mind you claim, choose, select, and arrive at decisions and conclusions. If you err in your judgment or decision, you experience the automatic or compulsory reaction from your unconscious mind. Your mind is always forgiving you, because the moment you present it with new mental imagery and lovely patterns of thought, it responds accordingly. It is perpetually forgiving you; this is called the love of God or the mercy of God.

The paralytic could not be cured until his sins had been cancelled; but once the inner state of mind is changed through contact with the Healing Power and his sense of oneness with It, he now rises through the Power of the Almighty (the One Power) and he no longer is carried around by four men, symbolic of worldly beliefs and erroneous impressions of all kinds. The outer change conforms to the inner, spiritual awakening.

And when they could not find by what way they might bring him in because of the multitude, they went upon the housetop. The multitude refers to man's mental accusers such as fear, self-accusation, remorse, and condemnation. When he realizes that Truth or God or the law of life never condemns, he ceases to condemn and forgives himself. Then instead of lying down prone in a bed of false beliefs and fears of all kinds, through his contact with the Almighty Power he stands upright in the law, visioning and imagining his perfect health and wholeness.

You must go on the *housetop* if you want an answer to your prayer. You must climb. You do this by reminding yourself of the One Omnipotent Power and your faith in It. We climb by faith; we soar aloft above our problem with wings of faith and disciplined imagination. Faith means to look up to the One, giving all your allegiance, devotion, and loyalty to God. Truth means to go in one direction only, knowing that the Great Physician is within, that He is healing you now, and that there is none to oppose, challenge, or thwart Him in any way. Fear is a denial of God and is nothing but a conglomeration of sinister shadows, without reality and with nothing to sustain it.

It is said they climbed up and opened the roof and let the paralytic down through the roof before Jesus. All this means is that in contemplating God and His Holy Presence, you are lifted up, your mind is open and receptive, and you let your deep, abiding conviction in the idea of perfect health sink down to subliminal levels within you. Jesus means God is your deliverer, the

I AM within you, which receives the impress of your conviction and responds accordingly. If you break the roof of a house, you can see the heavens above, the sun, moon, and stars. Don't let the press of worldly thoughts prevent you from receiving a healing. If your loved one is sick, open up the roof of your mind and let in the Healing Light, surrender your loved one to God and realize that he is now immersed in the Holy Omnipresence; see him as he ought to be, radiant, happy, and free. Claim what's true of God is true of your loved one. As you continue to do this, your loved one will rise up from his bed of pain, misery, and suffering, and walk the earth glorifying God.

And it came to pass also on another sabbath, that he entered into the synagogue and taught: and there was a man whose right hand was withered. And the scribes and Pharisees watched him, whether he would heal on the sabbath day: that they might find an accusation against him. But he knew their thoughts, and said to the man, which had the withered hand, Rise up, and stand forth in the midst. And he arose and stood forth. LUKE 6:6–8.

And looking round about upon them all, he said unto the man, Stretch forth thy hand. And he did so: and his hand was restored whole as the other. LUKE 6:10. *Related passage,* MARK 3:3–5.

Elsie H. Salmon, a Missionary's wife in South Africa, tells in her book *He Heals Today* about a child with a deformed left hand. Three fingers were missing and in their place were tiny stumps. After prayer there was a growth of the whole hand at the end of the arm, and they began to unfold like a flower in front of their eyes. She also states that there is absolutely no doubt in the minds of people who have followed developments that a perfect hand is forming.

We must not look upon this as miraculous or something supernatural. We must begin to realize that the Creative Power which forms, molds, and shapes the body can certainly grow a hand, a leg, or an eye. After all where do the organs of our body come from? If you made an ice-box, couldn't you fix it if it were out of order, or if broken, couldn't you mend it and supply the missing parts?

When Jesus said, *Stretch forth thy hand,* you must look upon it as a drama taking place in your own consciousness. You are Jesus in action when you know that the realization of your desire would save you from any predicament, be it what it may. You are Jesus or the spiritual man in action when your conscious and subconscious mind agree on the realization of your wish or prayer. When there is no further argument, and you have reached an agreement, you are Jesus Christ in action. Jesus represents your illumined reason, and Christ means the power and wisdom resident in your subjective self.

Elsie H. Salmon's faith in the Creative Power of God to form a new hand for a child caused the stunted arm to grow. Her faith is her savior or her Jesus. She is aware of the reality of what she prays for and knows that the nature of the Infinite Intelligence is responsiveness.

In the correct esoteric interpretation of the Bible, it must be understood that principles are personified as persons in order to make portrayal and interaction vivid and forceful. *Know ye not your own selves, how that Jesus Christ is in you, except ye be reprobates?* 2 Cor. 13:5.

We must not however confine the story of the man with the withered hand to its literal meaning. *The hand* is a symbol of power, of direction, of effectiveness. With your hand you fashion, mold, create, and design. *The hand* of the Almighty means the Creative Power of God focused or directed on some objective. Symbolically a man has a *withered hand* when he has an inferiority complex, feels guilty, inadequate, or is a defeatist. Such a man does not function efficiently and is not expressing his God-given powers.

We *stretch forth our hand* when we release our Hidden Power and become channels for Divine Love, Light, Truth, and Beauty.

His hand was restored whole as the other means a healthy, happy, well balanced, and wholesome personality. Numbers of people are sick, unhappy, dissatisfied, inept, and inefficient. Their attitude toward life is all wrong; moreover their work is shoddy and desultory. They do not sing in their hearts at their work. Whenever you turn with confidence and trust to the Almighty Power within knowing that you are guided, directed by this Inner Light, and that you are expressing yourself fully, you will actually become a channel for the Divine and you will move from glory to glory.

The dreams, ambitions, ideals, plans, and purposes of many are withered and frozen in the mind because they do not know how to bring them to pass. The external world denies their desire. Not knowing the laws of mind and how to pray scientifically, they find their wonderful ideas die aborning in their minds, resulting in frustration and neurosis. If you look around you in your office or factory, you will see many people with a *withered hand*. They are stagnating, literally dying on the vine. Life is progressive, life is growth. There is no end to our unfoldment or creativeness. We wither our hand (our ability to achieve and accomplish) by saying, "If I had Joe's brains or his wealth . . . his connections . . . I could advance and be somebody. But look at me, just a nobody. I was born on the wrong side of the tracks. I must be satisfied with my lot. I have a withered hand."

This is the way many people talk. They are constantly demoting and depreciating themselves. Liquidate, banish, and eradicate from your mind fear, doubt, and ill-will. Trust God completely, go all the way out on a limb and say with feeling and humility, "I can do all things through the God-Power and Awareness which strengthens, guides, comforts, and directs me." Watch the wonders you will perform. *Stretch forth your hand* by enlarging your concept or estimate of yourself. Aim high, raise your sights, realize you will always go where your vision is. You will be *stretching forth your hand* as you get a picture in your mind of what you wish to achieve. Touch this with faith in the God-Wisdom to bring it forth and you will see it made manifest on the screen of space. You will be satisfied for awhile; then a divine discontent will stir you again, causing you to aim higher and higher and so on to infinity.

To *stretch forth your hand,* when psychologically understood, is the soundest, simplest, and most wonderful philosophy any man can have.

I say unto you now, *Stretch forth thy hand.*

3

Absent Treatment and the Healing of Insanity

And when he was now not far from the house, the centurion sent friends to him, saying unto him, Lord, trouble not thyself: for I am not worthy that thou shouldest enter under my roof: Wherefore neither thought I myself worthy to come unto thee: but say in a word, and my servant shall be healed. For I also am a man set under authority, having under me soldiers, and I say unto one, Go, and he goeth: and to another, Come, and he cometh: and to my servant, Do this, and he doeth it. When Jesus heard these things, he marvelled at him, and turned him about, and said unto the people that followed him, I say unto you, I have not found so great faith, no, not in Israel. And they that were sent, returning to the house, found the servant whole that had been *sick.* LUKE 7:6–10. *Related passages,* MATT. 8:5–13. JOHN 4:46–53.

Here is the technique of absent treatment portrayed in a beautiful and simple way. You are told how to pray for another or send your *word* and heal him. When you pray for another, or give what is termed a mental and spiritual treatment, you simply correct what you hear and see in your mind by knowing and feeling the other's freedom. Faith comes to you as you leave the literal interpretation of life and enter into the psychological, spiritual interpretation of life.

Many of you, like the author, were no doubt in the United States Army and you know how to take orders. A soldier is conditioned to obey implicitly his superior officers. After considerable training the soldier becomes disciplined; *i.e.,* his mind and body are definitely bent to certain actions. The officer is a man of authority. He has learned to command, but first he had to learn to take orders himself; and he, too, is subject to authority from his superiors.

When you pray for another, you must be a good soldier; you must learn how to stand at attention and follow the order, "Eyes right." You must give attention to the spiritual values or Truths of life and keep your "eyes right" by seeing (spiritual perception) the other as he ought to be, happy, peaceful, and free. You must begin to discipline your thoughts, feelings, emotions, and faculties. You know very well that you can begin now as you read these lines. If your thoughts wander, bring them back and say to them, "I told you to give attention to health, peace," or whatever it is you are concentrating on.

The servants are your thoughts, ideas, moods, feelings, and attitudes of mind. They serve you nobly or ignobly, depending on the orders you issue. If you are an employer, you may order the employees to do certain things in the store. You expect them to obey; you are paying them to conform to your business methods and processes. In the same manner, you order your thoughts around. You are the master, not the serf or slave. Surely you do not and will not permit the gangster-thoughts of hate, fear, prejudice, jealousy, rage, etc., to order you around and make a football of you.

When you begin to discipline your mind, you do not permit doubt, anxiety, and false impressions of the world to browbeat, intimidate, and push you around. You are conditioning your mind so that you definitely issue orders to your thoughts to give attention to your aims in life, to your ideals; likewise, you direct and channel all your emotions constructively. You have complete dominion. You can't visualize an emotion. You must remember that emotion follows thought; and when you control your thoughts and mental imagery, you are in charge of your emotions.

No person, place, or thing can annoy you, disturb you, or hurt you—they do not have that authority. For example, another could call you a skunk. Are you a skunk? No. The suggestions or statements of the other could not affect you except through your thought. This is the only emotional power you have. Your thought in such an instance could be, "God's peace fills that man's mind." You are in charge of the movement of your mind. You can move in anger, hate, or revenge; also, you can move in peace, harmony, and good will.

The disciplined mind is accustomed to take a spiritual medicine called "In tune with the Infinite." The moment you are tempted to react negatively, identify immediately with your aim. Switch to your ideal immediately and you have overcome and are victorious. You are a man of authority, and you say to your thoughts (servants) *go and they go, come and they come.*

You can give your faculty of imagination to anything you wish, such as lack, loss, or misfortune. You can discipline, direct, and focus your imagination on success, health, and prosperity also. What you imagine and feel as true comes to pass. Let your imagination become the workshop of God, which is what it should be.

Let me cite the misuse of imagination. A mother whose son is rather late arriving home begins to imagine that he has met with some disaster. She sees in her vivid, distorted, twisted mind mental pictures of him on a hospital cot or she dramatizes an accident in her imagination. She can *send her word and heal him* and herself also. She must learn how to pray scientifically and become a good soldier who follows orders.

You are under *Holy Orders** when you pray. You have surrendered your ego and intellectual pride in your own thoughts, viewpoints, and perspective, yielding to the God-Wisdom within. You are under orders now to bring forth harmony, health, peace, joy, wholeness, and beauty in the world. You are here to let your light shine. You must have faith and complete trust in the Omnipotence, Omniscience, and Boundless Love of the Infinite which seeks only to express Itself. Identify yourself mentally and emotionally with God. You feel and know that you are a channel for the manifestation of all of God's attributes, qualities, and potencies, and that God flows through you as harmony, health, peace, joy, and abundance. As you make a habit of this kind of prayer by frequently repeating or affirming these Truths, your mind will become imbued with Eternal Verities, and you will find yourself under a Divine compulsion to bring forth only the good, the beautiful, and the true. You

---

* See my book *Prayer Is the Answer*, "Chapter five".

have placed yourself under *Holy Orders,* or Orders of the Only One—God. You become a God-directed man, a divinely ordained person whose sole mission in the world is to follow the orders of the *Holy One who inhabiteth Eternity whose name is perfect.*

Whose orders are you carrying out? *Ye are servants to whom ye yield yourself, servants to obey.* Whatever idea I yield to, or give myself to, will dominate, control, and compel me to act it out as frustration and expression.

In the above instance, whose order do you think the woman was obeying when she had all kinds of misgivings about her boy—bombarding him with a barrage of negation and with dire forebodings which if continued would have had catastrophic implications? This woman was taking her orders from the thoughts of fear, worry, and anxiety. In other words the marauders and intruders in her mind were browbeating her and making her a nervous wreck.

Begin now to *stretch forth your hand* by realizing there is no limit to your possibilities. Feel and believe God is your Silent Partner, counseling, directing, and governing you. As you do this, your life will be wonderful and satisfying. It will be more useful and constructive than it is. Begin to know yourself. Try the amazing power of true prayer as outlined in each chapter of this book. As you yield yourself to the

God-Wisdom, you will live a better life than you ever dreamed of.

Arise, take up thy bed (new mental attitude) *and walk* the earth radiant, happy, and free.

Now when he came nigh to the gate of the city, behold, there was a dead man carried out, the only son of his mother, and she was a widow: and much people of the city was with her. And when the Lord saw her, he had compassion on her, and said unto her, Weep not. And he came and touched the bier: and they that bare him stood still. And he said, Young man, I say unto thee, Arise. And he that was dead sat up and began to speak. LUKE 7:12–15.

Here is a wonderful, psychological drama. The *dead man* is your desire which you have failed to manifest. As you claim you now are what you long to be, you are resurrecting the *dead man* within you.

According to your belief is it done unto you. To believe something is to accept it as true. We are told the dead man was the son of a widow. A *widow* is a woman whose husband is dead. When we are not married, mentally and emotionally, to God and His truths, we are truly dead to peace, joy, health, happiness, and inspiration. A true widow is one whose husband is God, or the Good, and who is not governed by sense-evidence and worldly belief. The *son*, the desire, of such a woman will not remain dead because she turns to her Lord, which is the Creative Power within her and, with the door of her five senses closed, she completely rejects all that her senses deny. Silently and lovingly she claims and feels herself to be what she longs to be, knowing in her heart that her Lord (the Spirit within) will honor and validate her claim. She lives, moves, and has her being in the mental atmosphere of complete acceptance; as she continues to qualify her consciousness in this way, she reaches an inner conviction, thereby resurrecting the *dead man* within her. Her inner mood of triumph is her Lord commanding the *dead man. Young man, I say unto thee, Arise.*

This is the external manifestation of her subjective embodiment or the joy of the answered prayer. Whatever we appropriate and assimilate in consciousness, we resurrect. When it says the *dead man sat up and began to speak,* it means that when your prayer is answered you speak in a new tongue.

The sick man who is healed speaks in the tongue of joyous health and exudes an inner radiance. Our dead hopes and desires speak when we bear witness to our inner beliefs and assumptions.

As a corollary to this, I would like to relate about a young man I saw in Ireland a few years ago. He was a distant relative. He was in a comatose condition; his kidneys had not functioned for two days. I went to see him accompanied by one of his brothers. I knew he was a devout Roman Catholic and I said to him, "Jesus is right here now and you see him. He is putting his hand out and is this moment laying His hands on you."

I repeated this several times, slowly, gently, and positively. He was unconscious when I spoke and was not consciously aware of the presence of any of us. He sat up in bed, opened his eyes, and said, "Jesus was here; I know I am healed; I shall live."

What happened? This man's unconscious mind accepted my statement that Jesus was there and his subconscious projected that thought form; *i.e.*, this man's concept of Jesus was portrayed based on what he saw in church statues, paintings, etc. He believed Jesus was there in the flesh and that he had placed his hands upon him.

The readers of this book are well aware of the fact that you can tell a man in a trance that his grandfather is here now and that he will see him clearly. He will see what he believes to be his grandfather. His subconscious projects the image of his grandfather based on his subconscious, memory picture. You can give the same man a posthypnotic suggestion saying to him, "When you come out of the trance, you will greet your grandfather and talk to him."

He does exactly that. This is called a subjective hallucination. The faith kindled in the unconscious of my Catholic relative, based on his firm belief that Jesus came to heal him, was the healing factor. It is always done unto us according to our faith or mental conviction. The subconscious is amenable to suggestion even though the subject is unconscious; the deeper mind can receive and act upon the suggestion of the operator. In a sense you could call such an incident the *resurrection of the dead*. It is the resurrection of health, faith, confidence, and vitality. We must never let hope, joy, peace, love, and faith in God die in us; that state of mind is the real death. We should die to fear, ignorance, jealousy, envy, hate, etc. We should starve these states to death by neglect. When fear dies, there is only room for faith. When hate dies, there is only room for love. When ignorance dies, there is only room for wisdom.

Now it came to pass on a certain day, that he went into a ship with his disciples: and he said unto them, Let us go over unto the other side of the lake. And they launched forth. But as they sailed he fell asleep: and there came down a storm of wind on the lake: and they were filled with water, and were in jeopardy. And they came to him, and awoke him, saying, Master, master, we perish. Then he arose, and rebuked the wind and the raging of the water: and they ceased, and there was a calm. LUKE 8:22–24.

Here we are told how to control our emotions and heal the turbulent soul. This is a story of everyone, not just about men in a ship, because we are always traveling somewhere psychologically speaking. When beset with a difficulty, we seek an answer, a solution. When fearful, we must move to faith. The journey is always first in the mind the body follows where the mind goes. The body cannot do anything or go any place unless the mind agrees and directs. Consciousness is the only power and the only mover. The consciousness of man is perpetual motion. Our mind is always active, even when asleep.

Our *disciples* are our mental attitudes, moods, and faculties which go with us wherever we go. We must not let *Jesus go to sleep in the boat*. In order to understand the science of life in the Bible, you must regard—*Jesus*, the *boat*, the *wind*, the *waves*, and the *disciples*, as personifications of truths, faculties, moods, and thoughts of mankind. Your *Jesus* is your awareness of the Divine Power within you, enabling you to achieve, accomplish, and realize your objectives. Your knowledge of the laws of mind and your use of mental and spiritual laws is your *savior* or solution at all times, everywhere.

You must not permit *Jesus to sleep in the boat,* which means you must not go blithely along with the winds (opinions of man) and waves (fears, doubts, envy, hatred, etc.) of the race mind. The *lake* is your mind; when your mind is at peace, God's wisdom and God's ideas rise to the surface of your mind. The mind that stays on God feels God's River of Peace flowing through it and is full of poise, balance, and serenity. The *Storm* of *wind* represent the fear, terror, and anguish which seize man at times, causing him to vacillate, hesitate, and tremble with anxiety. He finds himself pulled two ways; his fear holds him back and prevents him from going forward.

What do you do when fear and limitation seize your mind? Realize that when you are looking at your desire, you see your *savior* or the solution in your mind. Your *savior* is always knocking at the door of your mind. Perhaps you are working for the government and you are saying, "Oh, I can't make any more money; I've reached the maximum." You are now seeing the *waters* of confusion and doubt welling up in you. Don't become submerged in these watery, negative emotions. Wake up your *savior*, stir up the gift of God within you.

Do it in this way. Realize first of all that the wish, desire, ideal, plan, or purpose you want to realize is definitely a reality of the mind, though invisible; then realize that by uniting with your desire mentally, you can definitely and positively move over the turbulent, noisy, and foaming waters of fear and hesitancy. Your faith is your feeling and your awareness that the thing you are praying for is a reality of the mind in the form of an idea or desire. Inasmuch as you thought about it, it is real. Trust the mental picture; it is real. By contemplating its reality you *walk over the waters* and you *quiet the waves of fear.* Your fear has abated because you know that when you focus your attention on your ideal, the Creative Power of God flows through that focal point of attention. You are now *stilling the waves.* You have disciplined your mind. You have reasoned it out and you know that the idea is always real. The thought is *the substance of things hoped for, the evidence of things not seen,* for the simple reason that you believe in the possibility of the execution of the idea.

Keep your eyes on your goal, your objective, knowing in your heart that there is an Almighty Power which supports you in all your ways. It never deserts you or leaves you. The subjective mind responds to your constructive thinking and feeling; thereby sustenance, strength, and power are given you. To look down at the *waves* of fear, false belief, and error is to sink. Look up and you will go where your vision is. Your ordered mind, your faith, and confidence enable you to walk over all the water of life to *green pastures and still waters.* You can *command the winds and waves,* and they will obey.

And when he went forth to land, there met him out of the city a certain man, which had devils long time, and ware no clothes, neither abode in any house, but in the tombs. When he saw Jesus, he cried out, and fell down before him, and with a loud voice said, What have I to do with thee, Jesus, thou Son of God most high? I beseech thee, torment me not. (For he had commanded the unclean spirit to come out of the man. For often-times it had caught him: and he was kept bound with chains and in fetters; and he brake the bands, and was driven of the devil into the wilderness.) And Jesus asked him, saying, What is thy name? And he said, Legion: because many devils were entered into him. And they besought him that he would not command them to go out into the deep. And there was there an herd of many swine feeding on the mountain: and they besought him that he would suffer them to enter into them. And he suffered them. Then went the devils out of the man, and entered into the swine: and the herd ran violently down a steep place into the lake, and were choked. When they that fed them saw what was done, they fled, and went and told it in the city and in the country. Then they went out to see what was done; and came to Jesus, and found the man, out of whom the devils were departed, sitting at the feet of Jesus, clothed, and in his right mind: and they were afraid. Luke 8:27–35. *Related passages,* Matt. 8:28–32. Mark 5:1–13.

In reading this account, it certainly reminds you of a manic-depressive type of psychosis. This is, of course, a form of mental derangement and is characterized by combativeness and destructivity. In the book of *Mark* we have a story similar to the above wherein the maniac is depicted as *living among the tombs.*

The *tombstones* are a record of the dead, which means here that the man is living in the dead past, nursing some old grudge or grievance until it becomes an obsession in his mind. The madman is a man who has allowed or permitted the gangsters of remorse, hate, revenge, or self-pity to take charge of his reasoning, discriminating mind. We must never abdicate and let destructive, negative emotions control us. Emotion follows thought; and by redirecting our thought life, we control our emotional life. Man cannot visualize an emotion. He has to construct the scene or event in his mind and relive it, thereby generating the emotion. In psychiatry the doctors endeavor to correct the basic conflicts of the patient and give him a new orientation.

Jesus addressing the insane man asks, *What is thy name? And he said, Legion: because many devils were entered into him.* I knew a man in New York who feared that whenever he went into a bar that some evil entity was lurking in the shadows somewhere to take possession of him. I don't know where he heard or read of such rank superstition. This belief governed his mind and caused all kinds of trouble. His subjective mind, being dominated by this all-potent but false suggestion, gained control of his reasoning faculties and his reason abdicated. He had to experience the effects of such a false belief; this subjective false belief gained the ascendency. He began to hear what he supposed to be spirit voices, not knowing he was talking to himself. He thought he was conversing with supernatural entities. He began to realize that his subconscious mind was simply acting in obedience to the false suggestions of fear and belief in spirits which he had dwelt upon so long. The subconscious will assume a dozen different characters whose collective name is *Legion*. This man went to a clergyman who used the ritual of the Church to banish the tormentors. The procedure of the exorcist was, as the reader will readily conclude, a series of incantations or adjurations in the name of Jesus Christ. The ritual, ceremony, and prayers of the exorcist instilled great faith and confidence in the subconscious mind of the man. He was very receptive to the power of the Church and the priest to cast out his so-called devils. The exorcist had confidence in what he was doing also. This coupled with the faith of the so-called possessed man brought about a marvelous healing. The priceless ingredient in the whole process was simply faith, which brought about a basic change in the mental attitude of the patient that generated a healing. It was, of course, blind faith which is certainly better than no faith at all. The bones of saints, certain waters, the incantations of a witch doctor may affect the deeper mind and cause a psychological transformation inducing faith and receptivity.

Divine healing or Spiritual healing refers to the harmonious functioning of our conscious and subconscious minds. Our mind contains within its conscious and subconscious areas all our desires, characteristics, tendencies, and urges with which we were born. Through the process of thinking, education, and experience we have acquired many attitudes and habits of various kinds. Man is a creature of habit. When we begin to think intelligently we deliberately reject all negative thoughts and opinions. When we fail to realize a desire or ideal, we become full of fear and frustration, this leads to unconscious impressions. These repressed urges and tendencies seek expression and an outlet. These destructive emotions manifest as inner conflicts; if those are not resolved, disorganization of the mentality takes place and a completely disordered mind is the result.

The subjective self in us is forever seeking to restore a balance in us; when our fears, tensions, and conflicts become unbearable, nature or the Divine Self in us causes us to lose all consciousness of the problems; this is called insanity. The mind is now deflected and detached from the strain and stress which caused the trouble. Imbalance results when we fail to choose between good and evil. We must not seek to solve our problems without Divine Wisdom and Divine Power. The mental derangement is simply the expression of deep, repressed urges and conflicts which are too great to bear. A complex is a group of ideas highly charged with emotion seeking expression.

If a man is full of hatred and prejudice, he is living in *the tombs*. When these are exposed and held up to the light of reason, they are dissipated. In Bible language, you are Jesus casting out the devils of hate, prejudice, and jealousy. These obnoxious complexes are always hiding in the *tomb* (subconscious mind). When men refuse to acknowledge and hold up their prejudices, peeves, and grudges to the light of reason, these ideas are forced down beneath the conscious level of personality and they are bound by the chains of fear, ignorance, and various mental obsessions. When we nurse grudges, prejudices, revenge, and remorse they sink into the unconscious area of mind like a smoldering fire ready to explode sooner or later. If we recognize these smoldering flames and handle them intelligently, we can be free and lead a normal life.

Our emotional side of life is the driving power. It would be a good thing for all of us to take a good look at ourselves and see if the qualities we criticize so harshly in others are not in ourselves. When our story says the insane man sat at the *feet* of the Master, it depicts our understanding of the laws of mind and how they work.

When you are asked to pray for an insane man in the hospital, you can't get his cooperation. He has ceased to reason and discriminate. Actually he is governed by the ghosts of the subconscious that walk the gloomy galleries of his mind. When you pray for such a type of person, it is necessary to do all the work yourself. You have to convince yourself of his freedom, peace, harmony, and understanding. You could pray two or three times a day in this way: "I now decree for John Doe that the intelligence, wisdom, and peace of God are made manifest in him and he is free, radiant, and happy. He is now clothed in his right mind. The Mind of God is the only Real and Eternal Mind; this is his mind, and he is poised, serene. calm, relaxed, and at ease. He is full of faith in God, in life, and all good things. I decree this, I feel it, and I see him whole and perfect now. Thank you, Father."

By repeating these Truths to yourself, realizing that there is but one mind, you will gradually, through frequent picturing in your mind, reach a dominant conviction; and the man you are praying for will at that moment be healed. In a case such as the above, all healing has to be done in the mind of the practitioner. The practitioner must not at any time give power to symptoms, or the prognosis of the case. He must rely exclusively on the operating Principle of Life which forever responds to his faith and trust in it. When you pray for another, you leave the realm of time and space, of appearances and circumstances, the verdict of the world, and you judge righteous judgment. This means that you come to a conclusion that the Inner Man (the Spiritual, Divine Presence) cannot be sick, confused, or insane. Nothing could ever happen to Wisdom, Peace, Harmony, Intelligence, or Divine Love. The inner man has all of these qualities and attributes, and the practitioner by meditating on the Eternal Life, perfect mind, and absolute peace of the mentally sick man, dissipates and dissolves the mist of fixed opinions and error thoughts that separate the man from God's River of Peace. Become aware now of the Almighty Power which is Invisible and Intangible. Don't struggle in your prayer-work; then you will find the outer coat of painting will fade away, and the masterpiece will be revealed in all its pristine glory.

The story says *the devils went out of the man and entered into the swine: and the herd ran violently down a steep place into the lake, and were choked.* Pigs were chosen symbolically as pigs decapitate themselves when swimming; likewise, when we begin to swim psychologically in the waters of life, our negative thoughts and confusions (devils) die from want of belief. The past dies for you when you no longer think of the past. If you feel you can't accomplish or cannot be healed, you are looking back at the past, you are living *among the tombs.* Don't listen to these messages of the past. The ideal or desire which beckons, which says to you, "Arise, go forth, achieve," is the savior walking down the corridors of your mind. Accept that ideal as real now and walk as though you possessed it. You are now *clothed* in your right mind, and a wave of peace moves over you because you realize that which you seek already is. This is why the Bible says, *Lift up your eyes, look on the fields; for they are already white to harvest.*

And, behold, there came a man named Jairus, and he was a ruler of the synagogue: and he fell down at Jesus' feet, and besought him that he would come into his house: For he had one only daughter, about twelve years of age, and she lay a dying. But as he went the people thronged him. And a woman having an issue of blood twelve years, which had spent all her living upon physicians, neither could be healed of any, came behind him, and touched the border of his garment: and immediately her issue of blood stanched. And Jesus said, Who touched me? When all denied, Peter and they that were with him said, Master, the multitude throng thee and press thee, and sayest thou, Who touched me? And Jesus said, Somebody hath touched me: for I perceive that virtue is gone out of me. And when the woman saw that she was not hid, she came trembling, and falling down before him, she declared unto him before all the people for what cause she had touched him, and how she was healed immediately. And he said unto her, Daughter, be of good comfort: thy faith hath made thee whole; go in peace. While he yet spake, there cometh one from the ruler of the synagogue's house, saying to him, Thy daughter is dead; trouble not the Master. But when Jesus heard it, he answered him, saying, Fear not: believe only, and she shall be made whole. And when he came into the house, he suffered no man to go in, save Peter, and James, and John, and the father and the mother of the maiden. And all wept, and bewailed her: but he said, Weep not; she is not dead, but sleepeth. And they laughed him to scorn, knowing that she was dead. And he put them all out, and took her by the hand, and called, saying, Maid, arise. And her spirit came again, and she arose straightway: and he commanded to give her meat. LUKE 8:41–55. *Related passages,* MATT. 9:20–22, 14:35–36. MARK 5: 28–34.

All these stories are psychological and must be interpreted as such. You are *Jairus* which means the ruling thought in the mind; *you throw yourself at*

Jesus' feet; *i.e.*, you begin to realize that based on your new understanding of the Power of God in you, you can resurrect the *dying child*. The *dying daughter* represents your unfulfilled ambition, the desire of your heart. *Jesus, Jairus*, the *daughter*, the *woman with the issue of blood, Peter, James*, and *John*—all these characters are within each of us. It is a story of everyman. Our *daughter* (desire) *is dying* because we lack the faith to resurrect it. A *woman with the issue of blood* cannot give birth, she cannot conceive. A bleeding womb cannot possibly give form to a body. *Woman* means emotion, feeling. When our emotions are running wild and undisciplined, we are symbolically *bleeding from the womb*. Energy and vitality are being wasted because of fear, worry, and doubt. The *womb* (mind) must be closed in order to procreate.

As you go within and shut the door of your senses to all objective evidence and assume that you are what you long to be, you are closing your *womb* (mind) and will succeed in giving form to your idea or plan. Your thought is creative; when you begin to think on what you wish to express, the Creative Power of God responds and by remaining faithful to the new mental focus, you will resurrect your child. You know in your heart that *the child is not dead* and that you can bring it forth. Your new attitude of mind which is your faith closes the *womb*.

Thy faith hath made thee whole. Faith comes through hearing that there is only One Sovereign and Supreme Power which can do all things for It is Almighty. As we give our attention to the Truth about this One Power, we are said to hear it. Let us hear the Truths about the Power of Love, faith, and good will, and let us trust our subjective wisdom to reveal to us the answer to any problem. Faith is going in one direction only. Many people give their ear or attention to lies, falsehoods, superstition, and erroneous concepts of all kinds. When we do this, confusion reigns supreme.

Somebody hath touched me: for I perceive that virtue is gone out of me. You can mentally and emotionally touch faith, love, joy, and peace. When you mentally appropriate the idea of perfect health, the Healing Presence responds, and you are made whole—this is the virtue that comes out of the depths of yourself.

We are told that *they laughed him to scorn.* Is it not true that your five senses mock and laugh at you? Do they not challenge you and say, "It can't be done," or "It is impossible." This is why you suspend your senses and direct your mind to give attention to the new mental picture, and as you envelop this desire with the mood of love, you become one with it. This is the meaning of taking *Peter, James, and John into the house with Him.* The *house* is your mind or consciousness. Your own I AM-NESS is the father and mother of all ideas, desires, concepts, and urges. *Peter* means faith in God; *James* means to judge righteously, *i.e.,* to hear the good news only; *John* is love or a sense of atonement, at-one-ment, with your ideal. We actually take these three qualities with us whenever we recognize a state as true that is not evident to the senses. Our reason and senses may question, ridicule, scoff, and laugh, but if we will only go within, knowing that when we feel something as true, Omnipotence moves in our behalf; then, though the whole world would deny it, we would demonstrate our desire because we are sealed in faith, and *according to our faith is it done unto us.*

4

Your Healing Presence

And, behold, a man of the company cried out, saying, Master, I beseech thee, look upon my son: for he is mine only child. And, lo, a spirit taketh him, and he suddenly crieth out; and it teareth him that he foameth again, and bruising him hardly departeth from him. And I besought thy disciples to cast him out; and they could not. And Jesus answering said, O faithless and perverse generation, how long shall I be with you, and suffer you? Bring thy son hither. And as he was yet a coming, the devil threw him down, and tare him. And Jesus rebuked the unclean spirit, and healed the child, and delivered him again to his father. And they were all amazed at the mighty power of God. LUKE 9:38–43. Related passages, MATT. 17:14–21. MARK 9:17–29.

There are similar stories in the *Book of Mark* and *Matthew*, which definitely seem to indicate a disease known as epilepsy today. Of course, looking at the story literally one would think of demon possession which was the popular belief in those days. The boy is thrown down; he foams at the mouth and wallows on the ground suffering from convulsions. The Bible does not mention the word epilepsy. The word is derived from the Greek word *epilepsia*, which means a falling sickness characterized by seizures. The Greeks called epilepsy the sacred disease because it was believed to be caused by the moon. As we all know, the term lunatic comes from the Latin word *lunaticus*. In ancient symbology the moon meant the subconscious mind. The sun was the illumined intellect or the conscious mind full of wisdom.

In other words the Bible is saying the child had a subconscious poison pocket which was the cause of his seizures and epileptic fits. *The sun shall not smite thee by day, nor the moon by night.* PSALMS. 121:6. Modern psychology and psychiatry show definitely that mental and physical disorders have their roots in the depths of the deeper mind, called the subconscious or unconscious.

Negative subconscious patterns are called *pestilences of the darkness.* By turning to the GodPresence within and calling on the Power and Goodness of God, we bring the action of God to play in our life. We prove our allegiance, devotion, and love for God by identifying ourselves with His qualities and by absolutely refusing to recognize evil as having any power over us. Because of our faith in the One Power, we claim His Perfect Harmony and Perfect Peace which is His Will.

Hippocrates, about 400 B.C., recognized this type of mental disorder called epilepsy which in his time was believed to be caused by divine beings. He ridicules the superstitions of his day and points out that the disease could not be of divine origin for the simple reason that the condition was healed by purifications and various incantations which were in vogue at the time. A local psychiatrist told me that his study of Hippocrates showed that this famous physician had a wonderful knowledge of the causes underlying mental disorders of all kinds.

Whether the child in question was an idiot child, deaf and dumb, or an epileptic doesn't matter. We must realize in praying for another that *with God all things are possible.* The *Book of Mark* says this type of case is healed by *prayer and fasting. Fasting* means, fasting from the sense evidence, symptoms, and race belief. We must *fast; i.e.,* mentally reject the poisoned feast of objective evidences.

Where did this healing take place? Jesus, as the story goes, had to heal himself of the disease, whether insanity or idiocy, and outer results necessarily followed. It is the *prayer of faith* which gets results. The mentally deranged state of consciousness is conditioned in us as long as we see that condition of illness portrayed. The failure to heal an insane child or an idiot is not the child's fault but the absence of faith in the *disciples* (mind's faculties). The one praying must cure himself of the claim supposedly gripping the ailing child; the condition is actually gripping the practitioner who is unawakened yet to the Truth. When we fail in this type of case, we simply have failed to fix our mind's eye on the embodiment of health which the ailing one needs.

We are told the reason the disciples could not heal the sick boy was due to unbelief. There is a deep unconscious belief in the minds of people that certain diseases are difficult to heal; when they see a lunatic and his symptoms, their senses are deeply impressed with the difficulties. The *disciples* spoken of are our own attitudes, mental faculties, and viewpoints. We must completely detach ourselves from the evidence of senses and identify with the Omnipotent Healing Presence, paying no attention to appearances and symptoms. Power, faith, confidence, and elevation of consciousness will come as we consider the Divine Masterpiece within and not the appearance.

Here is a treatment I use in treating mental disorders such as insanity, etc. I go within myself, mention the name of the patient; then I think of God for three or four minutes by mentally dwelling on Infinite Peace, Harmony, Divine Intelligence, Divine Love, and Wisdom. At the same time I claim that that which is true of God is true of the one I am praying for. I try to get the *feel* that all is order, harmony, bliss, peace, and joy in the mind of the person being prayed for. In this way I induce the mood or mental atmosphere of peace, health, and harmony. When I feel that I have done the best I can, I leave it and pronounce the person whole. I may repeat this treatment two or three times a day or as often as I am led to do so, always praying as if I had never prayed before. If I have only a partial realization, the person in question will feel better. The main thing is to keep on keeping on until the *day breaks and the shadows flee away* in your own mind.

The main purpose of all our prayers for others is to get the feeling of inward joy, and God will do the rest. In prayer we must go to *heaven*; that means a state of inner peace and rest. As we enter this *heaven* frequently, we shall see heaven on earth.

And he was teaching in one of the synagogues on the sabbath. And, behold, there was a woman which had a spirit of infirmity eighteen years, and was bowed together, and could in no wise lift up herself. And when

Jesus saw her, he called her to him, and said unto her, Woman, thou art loosed from thine infirmity. And he laid his hands on her: and immediately she was made straight, and glorified God. And the ruler of the synagogue answered with indignation, because that Jesus had healed on the sabbath day, and said unto the people, There are six days in which men ought to work. in them therefore come and be healed, and not on the sabbath day. The Lord then answered him, and said, Thou hypocrite, doth not each one of you on the sabbath loose his ox or his ass from the stall, and lead him away to watering? And ought not this woman, being a daughter of Abraham, whom Satan hath bound, lo, these eighteen years, be loosed from this bond on the sabbath day?
LUKE 13:10–16.

Healing by the laying on of hands has gone on for countless generations. I have seen some remarkable healings performed in that manner. Some say they are gifted and that their hands are *healing hands*. Of course if they believe that they have this divine gift of healing, it is done unto them as they believe. The truth of the matter is that all of us have the gift of healing. It is not a divine prerogative bestowed on the few. The Healing Presence is operating within you twenty-four hours a day. Did you ever consider all the cuts, bruises, and scratches you experienced when young? Did you not notice an Infinite Intelligence at work? It formed thrombin, closed up the cut, gave you new cells, and a complete healing took place. This happened in all probability without your being aware of it. The Intelligence within is constantly renewing your body. Faith causes this Healing Power to speed up tremendously, so much so that you can experience an instantaneous healing. As a matter of fact, a great number of churches of all denominations practice the laying on of hands.

We are told that the woman in the Bible story was healed on the *sabbath*. Many practice the *sabbath* from a literal standpoint, thinking it is a sin to drive a nail on the sabbath or do work of any kind. Some go to extremes and won't even handle money on the sabbath. All this is meaningless. *The sabbath* is an inner stillness, an inner certitude, whereby man reminds himself of the availability of the God-Presence in all emergencies, at all times, everywhere. You are *walking in the sabbath* when you accept in your mind that your prayer is answered. When you meditate and pray and succeed in reaching the point of inner peace; then your prayer is answered. You have reached the seventh day, the seventh hour, which psychologically means the moment of conviction. You are in the *sabbath* when your heart is aflame with the Glory of God and the certainty of His response, and at that moment you will experience an instantaneous, Divine transfusion of energy, power, vitality, and life.

We must realize that external acts, ritual, ceremony, and conforming to rites, precepts, and ordinances of some organization or church is not real religion or true worship. A man may observe all the rules and regulations of his church and at the same time violate all the laws of God in his heart. He could go to church every day of the week and yet be very unreligious. We must become aware of the fact that the only change that matters is the internal change, the change of the heart, where you have actually fallen in love with spiritual values; then all fear, enemies, and sickness will fall away.

When you walk in the consciousness of peace, health, and happiness, you are *in the sabbath* all day long. You are *in the sabbath* when you feel and know that it is impossible for your prayer to fail. You are unmoved, undisturbed, calm, serene, and tranquil because you are carrying in your subjective mind a divine impression, a subconscious embodiment of your ideal. You know that there is always an interval of time between the subjective embodiment and the objective manifestation. Your inner certitude and imperturbability is the sabbath, and *it was on the sabbath day that she was healed.*

The *ruler of the synagogue* mentioned in the Bible means the ruling thought or prevailing worldly viewpoint or opinion. *The synagogue* is your mind where the aggregation of thoughts, feelings, moods, and opinions gather. Jesus is always available, which means when you are looking at your desire, you are really looking at Jesus, or your solution, or that which saves. *The Woman who has the infirmity* means the feeling of weakness, the depressed state of consciousness, the subjective belief in some crippling disease. The word *woman* means emotional nature, the subjective side of life. Whatever our disease, it represents a negative pattern of thought, charged with emotion in our subliminal depths. The *ruler of the synagogue* represents the fear thoughts, the doubts, and arguments which come to your mind trying to dissuade you to turn away from the belief in the One Power which can do all things. There is an argument in your mind and you must psychologically slay these hypocritical thoughts, by asking them where they come from. Is there a principle behind them? Are they not shadows of the mind? The fear thoughts have no heavenly credentials. Take your attention away from them altogether and they die of neglect. Feast on God's Almighty Power, accept It, imagine that you are being healed now. Do this as often as necessary and you will experience *the sabbath,* or the fullness of acceptance; then you will rise and walk. *It is the sabbath day for you.*

5

The Incurable Are Cured

And it came to pass, as he went into the house of one of the chief Pharisees to eat bread on the sabbath day, that they watched him. And, behold, there was a certain man before him which had the dropsy. And Jesus answering spake unto the lawyers and Pharisees, saying, Is it lawful to heal on the sabbath day? And they held their peace. And he took him, and healed him, and let him go; And answered them, saying, Which of you shall have an ass or an ox fallen into a pit, and will not straightway pull him out on the sabbath day? And they could not answer him again to these things. LUKE 14:1–6.

The *Pharisee* is everywhere; he is the type of man who lays stress on external acts and observances. He adheres to the letter of the law and lacks the love and understanding behind the words of the Gospel. The

Pharisee believes that the fan gives him a stiff neck, that germs are the cause of his cold, and that the hidden virus is the cause of his influenza. The weather, conditions, and circumstances influence the mind in a suggestive way only. Man is the only thinker in his world; therefore it follows that the fan can't give him a cold except he thinks it does. A belief is a thought in the mind generally accepted as true. Many people can sit under a fan all day without getting a cold or a stiff neck. If one accepts the hypnotic suggestion that he will catch cold because of a draft, the fact still remains that the cold was due to his own thought. He had the power to reject or accept the suggestion. If accepted, the result is due to the movement of his own mind. He has no one to blame but himself. His mind accepted a false idea and produced the consequences.

The case of *dropsy* mentioned in the above Gospel story was due to a flood of negativity. When the mind is full of strain, stress, and tension, a corresponding effect is produced in the body, and there is a breakdown in the organs of elimination. If a man is possessed with hatred or deep-seated resentment, it could well bring on an internal flood which, if not checked, could terminate in disintegration of his vital organs due to the corrosive effect of these mental poisons. The conditions in the body are outpicturings of man's mental attitude or states of consciousness.

I knew a man in London who was very religious and completely free from any ill will or resentment. However, he saw his father die of dropsy, and it made a very deep impression on him; he told me that all his life he feared that the same thing would happen to him. He added that his father used to be tapped with an instrument and that the doctor would draw out large amounts of water from his abdominal area. This lingering fear, which was never neutralized, was undoubtedly the cause of his dropsical condition. He did not know the simple psychological truth which Quimby elucidated about a hundred years ago. Quimby said that *if you believed something, it will manifest whether you are consciously thinking of it or not.* This man's fear became a belief that he would become a victim of the same disorder that troubled his father. This explanation helped the man considerably. He began to realize that he had accepted a lie as the truth. The truth began to dawn on him that his fear was a perversion of the truth, a fear which had no real power because there is no principle behind discord. There is a principle of health, none of disease; a principle of abundance, none of poverty; a principle of honesty, none of deceit; a principle of mathematics, none of error; a principle of beauty, none of ugliness. His belief was the only power which controlled him. One's mind can be moved negatively or positively and can be influenced by good or evil.

This man saw the truth about his situation and cast out the lie. He reasoned that the Healing Power which made him was still with him and that his disease was due to a disordered group of thoughts; thus he rearranged his mind to conform to the Divine pattern. Before going to sleep at night he would affirm with feeling and with a deep meaning behind each word, "The Healing Presence is now going to work transforming, healing, restoring, and controlling all processes of my body according to its Wisdom and Divine Nature. I rest secure in this knowledge. I know it is God in action. There is no other power and this Healing Power is working now." He repeated this prayer every night for about thirty days. At the end of that time his mind had reached a conviction of health. This was the *sabbath day* for him, which meant the moment of complete fulfillment in his mind.

I attended a church service some years ago during which the minister gave a very fine talk on Divine Healing. After the service a member of the minister's church board said to him, "It's all right to say, 'Jesus healed', but don't say we can do it!" Can you imagine a statement like that in this so-called enlightened age? The man who said that had had hundreds of healings all through his life. Life is forever healing our cuts, bruises, sprains, and scratches. It never condemns us. When we take some contaminated food, the same

Life-Principle which seeks to preserve us causes us to regurgitate and tries Its utmost to heal us. A healing will take place if, as Emerson says, "we take our bloated nothingness out of the way."

I knew a Christian Scientist who swallowed a poisonous liquid by mistake one time. He was a splendid practitioner and had great faith in the God-Power. He told me that he was a hundred miles away from any kind of help so that he had to rely solely on the subjective power within him. He got very still and these are the words he used, "God is in His Holy Temple and His Presence fills every organ and cell of my being. Where God is there is only order, beauty, and perfect functioning. His Holy Presence neutralizes everything unlike Itself." He kept this up for an hour and, though in a very weakened condition, had a complete recovery.

Could one take a corrosive poison trusting the subjective power to nullify baneful effects? I don't suggest that anyone take on such a trial. I definitely believe that in an emergency or through a mistaken situation, the sincere truth student looking loyally to God for help could actually prove St. Mark's statement, *And if they drink any deadly thing it shall not hurt them*, and come out unscathed by the experience.

There are mental as well as physical poisons. The lawyers and the Pharisees are in all of us. They repre-

sent man-made laws and opinions, and the belief that
we are being punished for our sins, that our *karma*
is catching up to us, that we have sinned in a former
life, and that now we are expiating our sins. Pharisa-
ical thoughts come floating into our mind saying, "We
must not question God, maybe it is God's Will that we
be sick. This is the cross we must bear." Others have
a martyr complex and say, "God is testing me, this is
a trial. I must accept my suffering as the Will of God."

God's *Will* is the will of life, and life wants to
manifest itself as health, harmony, joy, wholeness,
perfection, and abundance. The Will of God is the
Nature of God, which is Boundless Love, Infinite Intelligence, Absolute Harmony, Perfect Peace, Infinite Joy,
Boundless Wisdom, and Perfect Order, Symmetry,
and Proportion. Life cannot wish death. Peace cannot
wish pain. Joy cannot wish sorrow. Harmony cannot
wish discord. Order cannot wish disorder. Love cannot wish punishment, misery, and suffering. People
who say that God is punishing them would never
dream of accusing or attributing to their own parents
the things of which they accuse God. To such people
the words *Infinitely Good* and *Perfect* seem to have no
meaning.

Many diseases follow such false beliefs for all our
beliefs tend to manifest themselves. To believe that
God is testing you or punishing you sets in motion the

law of your own mind bringing trouble, opposition, sickness, and difficulties of all kinds. That is why you hear a man say a jinx is following him. If man has a false premise, his conclusion or experience must conform with his false premise. Actually man punishes himself. He gives everything to himself, whether sorrow or joy, pain or peace.

Jesus means you, yourself, operating your conscious and subconscious mind synchronously and harmoniously. When you know the laws of your mind and apply them constructively, you are the Jesus of the Bible, raising the dead desires, healing the blind thoughts, and walking triumphantly toward your goal. You are no longer blind, halt, withered, or lame. This is why the Bible says, *And he took him, and healed him, and let him go.*

I have outlined for you in this chapter how a man healed a similar condition in himself. The same Healing Power is present in all men. It is not something that existed two thousand years ago. It is Omnipresent. You can lay hold of it and perform what we call miracles in your life. We must remember that a miracle cannot prove that which is impossible. It is a confirmation of that which is possible, always was, and always will be. For with God all things are possible.

Love, joy, and peace had no beginning and will have no end. Harmony always has been. The Principle of Life always has existed. It is not something that one man possessed. To say this would be the essence of absurdity. Don't wait for some angel or saint to heal you. Don't wonder whether God wants you to be healed or not. Realize that you are violating God's laws which are written in your heart and nature when you are sick, morose, hateful, or poor. Mental poisons are wrong thoughts which work underground in consciousness like a contaminated stream to emerge even after years of wrong experiences such as illness, loss, unhappiness, etc.

The first step in healing is not to be afraid of the manifest conditions from this very moment. The second step is to realize that the condition is but the product of past thinking which will have no more power to continue its existence. The third step is to *exalt the God who is in the midst of thee* (subjective self). This will stop the production of all toxins in you or your patient. You have now pronounced the condition false; in lifting yourself up, seeing the person as he ought to be, you draw the manifestation or the ideal state to you. Live in the embodiment of your desire and the *word* (your thought and feeling) will soon be made flesh. If you allow yourself to be swayed by the beliefs of man (mental poisons), you will not be able to live emotionally in your embodiment.

Among the most deadly mental poisons are the following: Hatred, which is really ignorance, and self-pity, which is really self-absorption. These drugs creep through the psychic bloodstream poisoning all springs of hope and faith, leading to dementia praecox, melancholia, and other forms of mental derangement. The spiritual antidote is to find your *other* real Self (God) and become God intoxicated. You can fall madly in love with the new knowledge that thoughts are things and that by filling your mind with spiritual values, you will transform your whole life, bringing you health, happiness, love, and joy. You can fall in love and become wildly enthusiastic in knowing that there is a Principle of Life which flows through your mental patterns and imagery creating after their image and likeness. When you realize that the law of attraction is forever operating in your life, you are seized with a Divine frenzy at the wonder of it all. You are now in love (emotionally attached) with God, or all things good, pleasing, elevating, and uplifting. You now hunger and thirst for more Wisdom and you move forward in the light of the One Who Forever Is.

Old age is another mental poison. The Bible looks upon age *not as the flight of years, but as the dawn of wisdom.* Seek the Divine Frenzy which cleanses you of all toxins. Like Daniel, even in the lions' den, exalt the God within you—the Divine Anti-Body.

6

The Healing Power of Thanksgiving

And it came to pass, as he went to Jerusalem, that he passed through the midst of Samaria and Galilee. And as he entered into a certain village, there met him ten men that were lepers, which stood afar off: And they lifted up their voices, and said, Jesus, Master, have mercy on us. And when he saw them, he said unto them, Go shew yourselves unto the priests. And it came to pass, that, as they went, they were cleansed. And one of them, when he saw that he was healed, turned back, and with a loud voice glorified God, And fell down on his face at his feet, giving him thanks: and he was a Samaritan. And Jesus answering said, Were there not ten cleansed? but where are the nine? There are not found that returned to give glory to God, save this stranger. And he said unto him, Arise, go thy way: thy faith hath made thee whole. LUKE 17:11–19.

This wonderful account of ten lepers being healed is a story of all of us. If you remove the stories of healings in the four Gospels, you have certainly emasculated one of the most important parts of the Gospels. The story of the lepers is telling all of us that sickness of the body has its origin in sickness of the soul.

I remember reading some time ago a report of a statement made by Dr. Elmer Hess as he was inaugurated president of the American Medical Association to the effect that a physician who does not believe in God has no business in a sick room. I believe that most physicians agree that faith in God has a profound effect in the maintenance of perfect health. Let us remind ourselves at this point of the famous saying, "The doctor treats the patient; God heals him."

As previously pointed out, the word *leper* in the Bible means a mind troubled with conflicting desires, emotions, and confused ideas. It means a sick mind, a man who is sick in his thoughts, his emotions, and his body. Leprosy is a wasting disease, therefore it typifies the state of a man who has lost his vitality, energy, enthusiasm, and vigor for life, because he has psychologically separated himself from the Source of all life. We have a leprous condition when we are full of envy, jealousy, anger, hatred, self-condemnation, etc.

When the Bible says *Jesus passed through Samaria and Galilee to reach Jerusalem,* it refers to a process of prayer or steps of prayer. Jesus represents the ideal, your desire, plan, or purpose which is always walking down the streets of your mind beckoning you onward and upward. Your ideal, picture, or vision is at this moment saying to you, "Rise up and accept me." When you raise your desire up in consciousness to the point of acceptance, you experience the truth of the statement, *Thy faith hath made thee whole.* Your desire must go through Samaria, which means confusion, double-mindedness, and conflict *in Galilee* (your mind).

The numeral *ten* mentioned here symbolizes the completion of a process. To look at it in a very simple way, the numeral one means the male or pressing aspect, namely your idea or desire. The naught or circle symbolizes a womb or receptive mind of man. *Woman* means the *womb of man.* In other words, *ten* means the interaction of the male and female elements of your own mind, thought and feeling, idea and emotion, the brain and heart. When these two are functioning harmoniously, constructively, and joyously, it is a happy marriage or union. Such a person is well integrated, healthy, vital, and courageous. The thoughts must be united with true feeling. Our thoughts must conform to the spiritual standard set forth by Paul, *Whatsoever things are true, whatsoever things are honest, whatsoever things are just, whatsoever things are pure, whatsoever things are lovely, whatsoever things are of good report; if there be any virtue, and if there be any praise, think on these things.* PHIL. 4:8.

True emotion follows true thought. The heart or subjective feeling nature should be the chalice of God's Love as it is the sanctuary of His Holy Presence. It is called the *cup* in the Bible. As we meditate on the spiritual values of life we receive a transfusion of love, faith, confidence, and energy which courses through our veins transforming our whole being. Our faith is kindled when we realize that all things are done by faith, which is a movement of Omnipotence within ourselves. There is only one power and that is our own consciousness. When we think of something, we have at that moment pin-pointed the flow of the Almighty Creative Power through one focal point of attention. Our faith is really our thought which, as Baudouin the French psychologist said, begins to execute itself immediately, taking form and function in your life.

All of us want to go to *Jerusalem,* the city of peace within ourselves, which means that when our desire is completely subjectified, we have reached the place of accomplishment or fulfillment. We are now at peace (Jerusalem). Our mind is no longer divided. The two (desire and faith) have become one and all is well.

The number *ten* is also a sacred number and bears reference to the line 1, and the circle 0, which produce a cross (X) only when there is a conflict in the mind. This conflict and frustration follows when man is in a double minded state. He has two powers and believes in good and evil. He looks at his environment, circumstances, and conditions and says to himself, "It's hopeless, all is lost, there is no way out of this dilemma, I'm incurable," and many similar statements. He is transferring the power within himself to external conditions, perhaps he is blaming the weather, other people, or a jinx for his trouble.

When desire and fear quarrel, the mind and the body become a battleground resulting in wasteful expenditures of energy, debility of the vital organs, nervous prostration, and exhaustion. Man must learn not to make a created thing or the manifested world a cause. He must not exalt the created thing above the Creator. He must resolve the conflict by going within himself and, like Quimby, placing his case before the Great Tribunal, God, the only Presence and the only Power. In the secret chamber of his own mind, he gives supreme recognition to the Spirit within. He looks at the fearful, negative thoughts and orders them out of his mind, realizing that they are only an illusion of power. There is no principle behind them and there is nothing to sustain them. He reminds himself that there is only one Creative Power and that It is now flowing through his thought-patterns bringing him the good he seeks. He keeps on doing this regularly and systematically until a healing of the situation takes place. He has reached a decision or pronounced judgment in his own mind. He has condemned the guilty cause (the negative thoughts) and has freed his prisoner (desire) into the arms of the Lord (his subjective self), where, through repetition, faith, and expectancy, his desire has sunk deeply into his subconscious mind. This is called depth therapy or as the Bible calls it, *entering Jerusalem* (*uru*—city, *salem*—peace), *i.e.*, reaching the point of conviction.

The cross we have been carrying is now removed because we have reached the place of death. Our desire has been entombed where it dies first; then comes forth as the answer to our prayer. The *word* (thought) has become *flesh* (made manifest in our body and environment).

The *cry of the ten lepers* is the cry of every man. It is the appeal of every troubled, frustrated, and neurotic person to the *Master* or Spiritual Power within, which alone can give peace and health of mind, body, and emotions. *They lifted up their voices.* You lift yourself up mentally when you turn in reverence, allegiance, and adoration to the Spiritual Presence within *who healeth all thy diseases. Master, have mercy on us.* The hundredth Psalm says, *His mercy is everlasting.* How beautiful are these words. They touch the heart strings causing you to go forth with the praise of God forever on your lips.

Go shew yourselves unto the priests. The word *priest* is a symbol of spiritual perception, an intuitive awareness of the great Truths of God. A priest is one who offers up a sacrifice. Every man is a priest of God when he turns away from the false gods and the poisoned feast of the irrational, mass mind with its fears, superstitions, and terrors in order to give his supreme attention to the one God and His Laws. He *sacrifices* or gives up his negative thoughts, fears, and false beliefs and contemplates love, peace, beauty, and perfection. He must give to receive. He gives up, *i.e.,* fasts from resentment and feasts on love; fasts from the idea of poverty and feasts on the idea of God's abundance; fasts from fear and feasts on faith in God and all things good; fasts from sadness and secretes the essence of joy, knowing that the joy of the Lord is his strength. The *true priest* fasts from pain and feasts on God's Silent River of Peace. He fasts from self-condemnation, depression, and self-pity, and feasts on amiability, sociability, kindliness, good will, and laughter. He fasts from symptoms and feasts on the mental vision of health and happiness. He fasts from darkness and feasts on the Light of God being reflected on all his problems, knowing the Light (intelligence) of God knows only the answer. He fasts from karma, fate, predestination, and feasts on God, the Eternal Now, knowing the Absolute does not condemn, judge, punish, or send sickness, disease, or death. He knows that though his hands are dripping with the blood of others and though he may have committed dastardly crimes, he can instantaneously turn to the Presence of God within, lifting himself up to the Heart of God, claiming and feeling that he now is the man God intended him to be, the happy man, the joyous man, the poised man, the peaceful man, the loving man. As this man paints a picture or vision in his mind and his heart, he hungers for an inward change; the Law of God automatically responds to his new mental pattern, and the past is forgotten and remembered no more. If man misused the laws of chemistry or electricity for twenty years, the moment he used the principle correctly the underlying laws of chemistry or electricity would automatically respond. The law cannot possibly hold grudges or try to get even. When we are dealing with our mind, we are also using the principle of mind. It makes no difference if you have been a murderer, a thief, or if you have committed all manner of evil, the moment you decide sincerely to change your life by enthroning a new concept and estimate of yourself in your mind and feel the truth of that which you affirm, the law reverses its former action and responds by corresponding to the new blueprint of your mind.

We must realize that the perfunctory prayer will not suffice. Only when sincerity and a new spiritual view of things takes hold of the mind do you expunge from your deeper mind the former negative patterns which caused all your trouble. You must remember that the law plays no favorites; moreover law is always impersonal. The laws of our mind never punish us. We merely experience the reaction of the law which we set in motion by our thoughts and beliefs. When man understands this, he has no occasion to hate or resent the meanest man who walks the earth. Furthermore, there is no basis for ill will, resentment, envy, or jealousy for all men may turn within for what they want. As they positively assert this claim for the good they seek, the law of mind responds to their mental acceptance. There is no basis for harboring ill feeling toward people who defraud or cheat us. There is nothing lost unless we admit the loss in our mind. All we have to do is to realize that all things exist in Infinite Mind, identify ourselves mentally and emotionally with that which we want, and our exchequer will again be replenished from the Infinite reservoir of God's riches in ways we know not of. There is no loss but the sense of loss. People who rob, defraud, or otherwise deceive us are merely messengers telling us who we have conceived ourselves to be. They testify to our state of consciousness. How could we be angry or hostile to others when they are merely instruments of our own mind, fulfilling the play which we wrote consciously or unconsciously in the book of life, our subconscious mind. It is easy to forgive; all we have to do is to forgive ourselves for having negative, destructive thoughts which hurt us, while those with whom we were angry probably have been fishing, dancing, or having a glorious time.

To heal any situation, *you show yourself to the priest*, for you are the *priest* yourself, forever giving up the lesser for the greater. You may offer your *sacrifice* now, which is your desire for a perfect healing, by directing your attention from the symptoms and the body, and dwelling with the Lord of Life within. Claim that the Infinite Healing Presence is saturating every atom of your body, making you whole, pure, and perfect. Know and feel that the Living Intelligence which made your body is now taking over, causing all the organs of your body to conform to God's eternal pattern of harmony, health, and peace. As you enter into the mental atmosphere of harmony, health, and peace, a rearrangement of your thought-patterns takes place followed automatically by molecular changes in the body structure to conform to the new state of consciousness. You are now transformed because you have had a spiritual transfusion of the Healing Power released by your prayers so that every atom of your being dances to the rhythm of the Eternal God.

Were there not ten cleansed? but where are the nine? The numeral nine mentioned refers to the consciousness of possession. Possession is nine points of the law when we enter into the feeling of being what we long to be, or as we continue to claim and feel as true that which we affirm; we add thought to thought, mood to mood, and finally we reach the point of fulfillment in consciousness. The next step is *ten*, or our good made manifest. The cycle of consciousness has been completed; we are back where we started. We began thinking of God (the One), and we ended experiencing God (the One). Everything resolves itself back to ONE, its starting point. You glorify God each time your prayer is answered. Your thought and feeling become one as they are fused together by enthusiasm and love. The *issue* is the son in expression, the idea objectified.

It is said the one who gave thanks was a *stranger.* The *stranger* in your mind might be sickness, fear, worry, or a business difficulty. These negative attitudes are *strangers,* aliens in the house of God. Our mind is supposed to be a house of prayer, not a den of thieves. Fear, worry, and anger are the *strangers* and intruders who rob us of peace of mind. When we starve these states through neglect, by giving all our attention and devotion to God and His Attributes and Qualities, our mind is cleansed. At that moment we are praising and exalting the God in the midst of us.

And one of them, when he saw that he was healed, turned back, and with a loud voice glorified God, And fell down on his face at his feet, giving him thanks. Here is a perfect formula of prayer. You may be expressing yourself in a wonderful way, be happily married, have a very prosperous business, have wonderful friends, yet, you may have a bad heart or have trouble with your eyes.

There was a man in our recent class on the *Book of Job* who wrote me saying that he was leaving the nine harmonious, stable conditions of his life to fill up the one that was lost or missing. He said that he went to work on a quality in which he was sadly lacking, namely, thankfulness. This young man said he rarely praised anybody and that he was not thankful for all his blessings. He was amazed when he began to consider all the wonderful things that happened to him and the many blessings he enjoyed. The *stranger* in his midst was eye trouble. The mood of gratitude and the thankful heart causes us to tune in with the creative forces of the universe and what we send out comes back to us multiplied by the law of action and reaction.

This young man quieted the wheels of his mind and began to imagine he was talking to the King of

Kings, the Lord of Lords within himself. He had no mental picture of God, of course. In his mind's eye he sensed that the Divine Presence was there, the very Life of him. He began to say, over and over again, "Thank you Father, Thank you Father." He kept repeating this softly, quietly, gently, and lovingly. He was in a sleepy, drowsy, state each night as he meditated in the manner outlined. He would go to sleep in the mental mood of thankfulness. He had a perfect healing of his eyes. In biblical language *he fell down on his face at his feet.* The word *face* means the Truth and Presence of God; *feet* mean understanding. *To fall down* is to humble yourself and set aside the intellect, knowing that Infinite Wisdom and Power are within and can do all things. He understood that vision is spiritual, eternal, and indestructible, and that all he had to do was to enter into the mood of thankfulness for the gift already received. The grateful heart is the mind which believes and rejoices in the joy of the answered prayer. You have oftentimes thanked the man behind the counter for the coat, wrap, or suit which you paid for, but did not receive. You know that he will send it to you and you trust him implicitly. God's promises never fail and you can also give thanks for the gifts which have already been given you. Rise to the point of acceptance and go forth with a grateful heart for the gift already received.

I have been a stranger in a strange land. Ex. 2:22. All of us are really wanderers, pilgrims, and strangers here. We have left Paradise and do not feel at home here. Our pilgrimage is back to the One. We have loves, urges, ideals, and aspirations; and as we look at the world, it seems to deny the inner whisperings and murmurings of our heart strings which remind us of our origin and urge us back to it.

There is only one thing to do; there is only one thing all men are seeking, and that is the God within, the Creative Presence and Power. Leave the good, sound qualities, aspects, conditions, and circumstances of your life and find the *stranger*, the thing that bothers you, that is at present annoying you. Some desire perhaps is not fulfilled. Turn to God within and still the wheels of your mind; immobilize your attention, focus your mental lens on the fact that the Spirit within you, God, is the Cause and the Source of all your good. Then give thanks by silently repeating, "Thank you," over and over again as a lullaby, until your mind is full of the feeling of thankfulness. Continue to do this until you are filled in consciousness. The moment you qualify or condition your consciousness, the answer will come. The *lepers* are now cleansed. Let your prayer be "O God, give me one more thing, a grateful heart."

7

Eyesight Restored

And it came to pass, that as he was come nigh unto Jericho, a certain blind man sat by the way side begging: And hearing the multitude pass by, he asked what it meant. And they told him, that Jesus of Nazareth passeth by. And he cried, saying, Jesus, Thou son of David, have mercy on me. And Jesus stood, and commanded him to be brought unto him: and when he was come near, he asked him, Saying, What wilt thou that I shall do unto thee? And he said, Lord, that I may receive my sight. And Jesus said unto him, Receive thy sight: thy faith hath saved thee. And immediately he received his sight, and followed him, glorifying God: and all the people, when they saw it, gave praise unto God. LUKE 18:35–43. Related passages, MARK 10:46–52.

There is the well known, duly authenticated case of Madame Bire. She was blind, the optic nerves were atrophied, useless. She visited Lourdes and had what she termed a miraculous healing. Ruth Cranston, a Protestant young lady who investigated and wrote about healings at Lourdes in *McCall's Magazine*, November, 1955, writes about Madame Bire as follows: "At Lourdes she regained her sight, incredibly, with the optic nerves still lifeless and useless, as several doctors could testify after repeated examinations. A month later, upon re-examination, it was found that the seeing mechanism had been restored to normal. But at first, so far as medical examination could tell, she was seeing with 'dead eyes'."

I visited Lourdes in 1955 where I, too, witnessed some healings,* and of course there is no doubt but that healings take place at various shrines throughout the world, Christian and Non-Christian.

Madame Bire, to whom we just referred, was not healed by the waters or by the Shrine, but by her belief. The healing principle within herself responded to the nature of her thought. Belief is a thought in the mind. It means to accept something as true. The thought accepted executes itself automatically. Faith means to accept that what you are praying for already

---

* (See chapter 1 in my book *Traveling With God*.)

is. Undoubtedly Madame Bire went to the Shrine with expectancy and great faith, knowing in her heart she would receive a healing. Her deeper mind responded to her belief and Spiritual forces were released, restoring her vision according to her belief. *According to your belief is it done unto you.* The Healing Presence which created the eyes can certainly bring a dead nerve back to life. What the Creative Principle Created in the first place, It can recreate.

Healings occur sometimes unheralded at various religious services. Some people have told me that they had healings at our healing service on Sunday mornings. They add that they did not expect a healing, that they were skeptical, that they were in no state of exaltation, and were not even thinking of a healing. From what they say one would gather that they lacked faith; therefore the question arises, how could they receive a healing? The answer is rather simple. They are looking for a healing and their minds are open and receptive to receive the prayers of the multitude present. Perhaps they are going to a doctor, osteopath, or chiropractor for treatment, which is highly indicative that they desire to be healed. Desire is prayer; this attitude indicates a very receptive mind for the idea of perfect health to be resurrected, for which the people present are praying. When a group of people, gathered together in prayer, affirm that all those who are present are healed, made whole and perfect, they are establishing a definite psychological and spiritual link among all those present; then even if unbelievers or skeptics are present, it is possible for them to be healed for the simple reason that they desire a healing.

You might ask the question, "What about a person who is full of hatred, ill will, and resentment, would he get a healing at a Shrine or at any church healing service?" If the faucet or a pipeline is full of debris of all sorts, the water will not flow freely; furthermore, the water will be muddy and contaminated. It is necessary to remove the kinks in the hose when watering the garden. Your body is the garden, and when you pray you are watering your garden with the Healing Power of God. The healing waters are love, peace, joy, faith, good will, confidence, and strength. The man full of hate is opposed to the stream of love and joy. He must decide to let go of his grudges and pet peeves, and to let in the sunshine of God's Love. His mental block sets up a resistance to the Healing Principle and a short circuit takes place. When he lets down the bars, the invasion of love and grace can penetrate. A person who refuses to resolve his mental conflicts definitely delays his healing. The consciousness of love is the most potent healing force in the world. The doctor, priest, rabbi, or New Thought minister possessing the greatest measure of God's Love will get the best results.

Jesus said to the blind man, *What wilt thou that I shall do unto thee? And he said, Lord, that I may receive my sight.* The beggar was specific because he knew what he wanted and said so. Life is always asking you, *what wilt thou of me?* What is your desire? Millions of people are blind; *i.e.,* they are psychologically and spiritually blind because they do not know that they become what they think all day long. Man is spiritually blind when he hates, resents, or is envious of others. He does not know that he is actually secreting mental poisons which tend to destroy him.

Thousands of people are constantly saying that there is no way to solve their problems, that the situation is hopeless. Such an attitude is the result of spiritual blindness. Man begins to see spiritually and mentally when he gets a new perception of the mind, knowing that there is an Infinite Intelligence within him that is responsive to his thought which can solve all problems. The cry of the world is, "I want my sight." Men, women, and children should receive their sight. They should be taught in schools, in colleges, and in homes throughout the land, where the Creative Principle of Life is and how to use it. They should be taught the interrelationship of the conscious and subconscious mind.

Emerson said, "A man is what he thinks all day long." The Bible says, *As a man thinketh in his heart so is he.* Men should be taught that the Principle of Life is responsive to their thought and that when they claim that Infinite Intelligence leads and guides them, revealing to them the perfect answer, they find themselves automatically led to do the right thing as the way opens up. They were once *blind* to these truths; they now begin to see the vision of health, wealth, and happiness, and peace of mind.

And Jesus said unto him, Receive thy sight: thy faith hath saved thee. Jesus symbolizes the Redeemer or the Healing Principle of Life within all of us which forever responds to our expectancy or faith. Your faith is your feeling, your awareness, your inner conviction that what you are praying for already is. Vision is eternal, spiritual, and indestructible. We do not create vision, we manifest or release it.

Recently a woman came to me with incipient glaucoma, which is hardening of the eyeball. I read some time ago an article which stated that ophthalmologists in one of the larger hospitals discovered that there was a pattern of hatred in about twenty to twenty-five per cent of the cases of glaucoma in the hospital. This is not true in all cases, of course. In others who indulge in negative or destructive thinking, the liver, heart, lungs, or other organs may be affected, depending on the susceptibility of the person. The disease may also be due to fear, or race mind impinging on the consciousness of people who fail to pray. This woman began to pray for a daughter-in-law whom she hated intensely. She did it this way: "I release _____ unto God. I wish for her all of God's happiness, peace, and joy." She repeated this prayer frequently until all the roots were withered in her mind. Actually she began to feel kindly toward the daughter-in-law after a few weeks.

This is how true love melts everything unlike itself. We prayed together frequently; we were *en rapport* with each other. All of us are sending and receiving stations. She was open and receptive to the truth, and she prayed frequently using the prayer "Perfect Eyesight" in one of my books of meditations* which is as follows:

"My eyes are God's eyes, and I see perfectly. The Living Intelligence which made my eyes is now controlling the processes and functioning of my eyes and my entire body. I know and believe that my vision is spiritual, eternal, and indestructible. "If, therefore thine eye be single, thy whole body shall be full of light." This means I see only the Truth; I love the Truth; I know the Truth. I see God in all men and in all things. I see spiritually, mentally, and physically. My eyes reflect the glory, the beauty, and the perfection of God. It is God looking out through my eyes seeing His

---

* (See my book *Quiet Moments With God.*)

own ideas of perfection. My eyes are the windows of my soul; they are pure, and are kept single to Love, Truth, and Beauty at all times. The harmonizing, healing, vitalizing, energizing Power of the Holy Spirit permeates every atom, cell, nerve, tissue, and muscle of my eyes making them whole, pure, and perfect. The Divine, perfect pattern is now made manifest in my eyes, and every atom and cell conforms to God's perfect pattern on the Mount. Thank you Father."

She let these truths sink down by a process of spiritual osmosis into her deeper mind and gradually a perfect healing took place. She cooperated perfectly with her doctor, praying for him also. At the end of a few months, she had no longer any occasion for the eye drops. The doctor said all tension had disappeared.

I know many people who have had miraculous results with the following simple prayer. "I see spiritually; I see mentally; I see physically; It is wonderful." They fill their soul (subjective nature) with the sense of wonder, and wonders happen when they pray. Jesus, Moses, Elijah, and Paul could not use any other Healing Principle than the one you are using. It is the same yesterday, today, and forever.

When our thought-patterns are disorganized, we are sick. Our dark, dismal thoughts hide the vision of our God. When we pray by identifying ourselves with the eternal, spiritual values, a rearrangement of our thought-patterns takes place followed by a molecular change in the body which conforms with the changed mental attitude. The healing follows. Sight is displayed, not created.

If deaf, we hear again the sound of He Who Is. We realize It is God hearing His own sound through His own ears. It is God seeing His own perfect ideas through His own eyes. The woman who was healed of glaucoma had faith and knowledge; she will, of course, have no return of the disease. The healing will be permanent.

A blind faith will bring a healing, but ofttimes it is impermanent and fallible. Keep your mind fixed on God and His Perfection and your healing powers will be more proficient and successful. As you walk the earth in quiet moments with God, you will be practicing His Presence and releasing His Healing Power all the time without even knowing it.

Remember we see *through* the eye, not with it. The cornea of the eye receives vibrations from objects in space; through the optic nerve these vibrations are carried to the brain. When the inner light or intelligence meets the outer light, we see. "We see because the Seer is within." We see because Infinite Intelligence is the light of our consciousness. If your eyes are not functioning perfectly, the Creative Principle which made them hasn't been hurt or injured. He that made your eyes can also recreate, refashion, and heal them. *Behold, I make all things new.* Your eyes symbolize Divine Love, a delight in the ways of God, and a hunger and thirst for God's Truth. You will always have good vision if you tune in to the Love of He Who Is. The *right eye* symbolizes right thought and right action. The *left eye* symbolizes God's Love and His Wisdom. Think right, radiate good will, and you will focus perfectly.

You can receive your sight. Yes, you can perceive the answer to any problem, be it what it may, by recognizing the Source of all good. Give supreme allegiance to the God-Presence within and feel the reality of what you are praying for. You don't go to God with a problem. You come to God giving thanks for the answer which is yours now as you open your mind to receive.

Receive thy sight. And immediately he received his sight, and followed him, glorifying God.

8

Hearing Restored

*A*nd one of them smote the servant of the high priest, and cut off his right ear. And Jesus answered and said, Suffer ye thus far. And he touched his ear, and healed him. LUKE 22:50–51.

Many people ask me whether it is right to pray for someone who is sick, troubled, or in some difficulty. Then they usually say, "He didn't ask me to pray for him." As you read the above verses, you are not told that the servant asked Jesus to restore his ear. Jesus apparently didn't wait for the question, but voluntarily restored the ear. It seems like begging the question to ask, "Should I pray for someone in trouble?" Of course you may pray for anyone you wish, and it would be most excellent to pray once a day for all men throughout the world, wishing them harmony, health, peace, and joy. Pray for the President, the Congress, people in your office, your home, and the whole world will be blessed because you have performed such unselfish devotions.

Sometimes I am asked this question, "Should I pray for my mother who does not believe in Divine Healing and is opposed to this teaching about mental and spiritual laws?" The answer is simple. If the mother, father, or relative has no faith in your religious convictions or in your particular technique or process of prayer, that does not make any difference whatever. When you pray for someone, you must not bother with the question of whether he believes or disbelieves, whether he accepts or rejects. Neither do you concern yourself with his church affiliations or his agnosticism; furthermore you pay no attention to his symptoms, aberrations, mental conflicts, or blocks of any kind. You simply enter into the silence of your soul, immobilize your attention, and mentally reject all sense-evidence. You do this decisively and categorically. Quietly know that the Infinite Healing Power is timeless and spaceless and that It embraces the one you are praying for; then you silently feel or quietly affirm the Truth, just as you like. You don't have to use any words. You can feel the Truth of what you think, that the Harmony, Health, Power, Peace, Order, and Perfection of God are now being manifested in your friend's mind and body. Know that there is but one mind, and in mind there is neither time nor space. You are one with your friend, because you are thinking of him. In the language of Troward, you are *en rapport* with him, and in the language of Quimby, you are one with him, because our minds mingle like atmospheres and each has his identity in that atmosphere. What you feel and know as true about your friend will be resurrected in his experience. You have taken his request, or his desire for health, and made it your own.

As you contemplate the qualities and attributes of God, knowing that these qualities are now being experienced by your friend, there is an immediate response in the mental structure of your friend, and a reordering of his mind takes place bringing about a perfect healing. Your inner sense of peace and confidence that the law of health and harmony is now in operation brings about a sense of faith and trust in you. As you continue to pray, perhaps two or three times a day, the time will come when you will lose all desire to pray because your prayer is answered. You can't desire what you have. A doctor does not treat a patient who is healed; the patient requires no further treatment. Prayer operates on the same principle. You pray until you need no longer pray.

We see and hear with the mind. In biblical language *we cut off an ear* when we cease listening to the troubled voice of the world with its false beliefs, terrors, and superstitions. *Jesus touching the ear and healing it* means that we should hear the voice of Truth which says, *I am God and there is no God beside me.* We should hear only that which fills our soul with joy. Hear the good news about the other. To what are you giving attention? If you are listening to gossip, criticism, and condemnation, you are not hearing the Truth. If someone tells you that you are going to fail in your enterprise and if you give him any attention, you are not hearing the gospel or good news about yourself.

Go within yourself, place all your attention on the idea of success. You will immediately begin to enter into a mood or feeling of success. You are now hearing the good news because you are under a good spell. You are now absorbed, engrossed, and fascinated by the idea of success, achievement, and accomplishment. You know that fear and success are simply two ideas in the mind. You know that you were born to succeed, and that you have all the equipment necessary. The fear-thought is false, it's an illusion, it's a shadow of the mind. A shadow has no power or substance. The idea of success is real and your subconscious powers will move on your behalf, compelling you to take all the steps necessary, as you give your attention to the idea of success. You are now hearing the Truth. It is always right to bless the other. Surely there can't be anything wrong with wishing for the other person health, harmony, joy, peace, and all of God's riches. That is the answer to those who say, "Is it wrong to pray for the other if he didn't ask me?" Of course not. You should wish for everyone what you wish for yourself. Love is the fulfilling of the law. Love is sincerely radiating the sunshine of God's Love, Light, and Truth to all men everywhere. This is the Law which brings fulfillment, happiness, peace, and abundance into your own life. What we withhold from another, we withhold from ourselves. Actually there is no other, all of us are in the One Mind and the One Spirit which is Indivisible. There can be no divisions or quarrels in It. One part can't be antagonistic to another part. If that were so there would be no harmony, only chaos. The Infinite cannot be divided.

For example, if you are praying for prosperity and you are resenting the wealth and riches of another, you are condemning what you are praying for, and your good takes wings and flies away. How can you attract wealth when you resent its manifestation in another. You are thinking and feeling lack instead of abundance, and as you think and feel, so are you. Thinking makes consciousness, and your state of consciousness governs your world. When you see this Truth, you are *Jesus* (illumined reason, awareness of truth) *touching the ear* (hearing the truth which frees you) and *healing it, i.e.,* bringing about a state of wholeness or unity in your mind.

You are told that *he cut off his right ear.* The *right* means the objective world, worldly opinion, sense evidence, and judging according to appearances. *Cut off that right ear now,* once and for all, and give no power to external phenomena. Do not worship or give power to germs, nor bow down in fear before them. Don't get panic-stricken when someone sneezes and say, "Oh, I'll catch a cold." Reject the false belief that a fan will give you a stiff neck, or that the cold night air will give you pneumonia or cause bronchial trouble. The weather has no power over you. We give power to these things because we believe that they affect us; we suffer according to our belief. The fan is harmless, it never said to anyone, "I will give you a cold if you sit near me or under me." The fan is neutral. It is a metallic substance, composed of molecules revolving at a high speed. Bless the fan, bless the weather; God pronounced all things good. When your feet get wet, don't say that the water will give you pneumonia. The water never said that, why do you say it? Man has created countless false gods; and all his trouble arises out of his darkened mind and distorted imagination.

Nicoll of England says that all man's evil is due to misunderstanding. Man sees *through a glass darkly,* due to the twilight in his mind. When the shadows fall in the evening, sometimes man mistakes a stump of a tree with some branches for an enemy with a gun aimed at his heart. He becomes frozen with fear. This is the twilight in his mind. He has not heard, he has not seen. Become Jesus; *i.e.*, become awakened to the Truth and know that there is but one Primal Cause which is your own Consciousness; cease making secondary Causes. To know that your I AM is the only Power, the only Cause, the only Substance, is to free you from all the false gods of the world, enabling you to go forth with the song of God in your heart.

Your *ears* are symbolic of understanding. Many people who complained of their inability to hear the writer at his public lectures on Sunday now sit at the rear of the lecture hall and hear perfectly. Their interest in Truth was aroused; their attention was quickened; and there was a normal, healthy response from the deeper mind. The following is a simple prayer which I give to people suffering from ear troubles of any kind:* "I hear the Truth; I love the Truth; I know the Truth. My ears are God's perfect ideas functioning perfectly at all times. My ears are the perfect instruments which reveal God's harmony to me. The Love, Beauty, and Harmony of God flow through my ears;

---

* See my book *Quiet Moments With God*.

I am in tune with the Infinite. I hear the Still, Small, Voice of God within me. The Healing Presence quickens my hearing and my ears are open and free."

My experiences with people have convinced me that a great number of people become deaf, or partially so, because they don't want to hear the voice of someone. They are trying to shut out certain things. If a man has a nagging wife, he may not want to hear her, and gradually he loses his hearing capacity. These negative auto-suggestions sink into his subconscious mind, and the latter proceeds to follow out the suggestion given. You can place man in a trance state and suggest to him that he can't hear until you tell him he can. The subconscious, being amenable to suggestion, accepts the suggestion of the operator and he can't hear; this shows us how our mind works. We must, therefore, be exceedingly careful of the thoughts we entertain and give attention to in our mind.

There are many people who deliberately shut out the Truth. They say, "I don't want to hear a word of that. Shut that man off, I don't want to hear his voice. I hate that voice. I don't want to hear it. I won't hear it," etc. These and similar statements are expressed with such emphasis and feeling that they become highly destructive. Our subconscious mind accepts these statements as requests, and proceeds to bring them to pass in our experience. You have heard the old maxim which contains a great Truth, "There are none so deaf as those that will not hear."

Dr. Flanders Dunbar, famous authority on psychosomatic medicine, cites many cases where deafness was due to mental and emotional disturbances. In her book *Emotions and Bodily Changes,* she cites a case of a man of forty-five who had been married for twenty years and had to use a hearing aid. He ascribed his deafness to swimming. He thought that one advantage of being deaf was that he didn't have to listen to his wife. The doctor asked to examine the hearing aid, but went right on talking. They became engaged in such an animated conversation that it was not until half an hour later that he discovered the doctor was still holding his hearing aid. By now, of course, you have deduced what was wrong with his hearing. His subconscious mind responded to his desire not to listen to his wife. There are people who have a form of deafness due to the fact that their mind is closed to all ideas but their own. They are unyielding, inflexible, dogmatic, and full of pride.

Hearing is a mental and spiritual process. Trust the Divine Intelligence which made your ears and all their parts. *I will restore health unto thee and heal thee of thy wounds saith the Lord.*

9

Prayer Wipes Out All Karma

We have finished with the miracles of healing reported in the book of *Luke*, which have parallel accounts in *Mark* and *Matthew*. The book of *John* is the most mystical book in the Bible. In the ninth chapter of *John*, a story is told of a man *which was blind from his birth.*

And as Jesus passed by, he saw a man which was blind from his birth. And his disciples asked him, saying, Master, who did sin, this man, or his parents, that he was born blind? Jesus answered, Neither hath this man sinned, nor his parents: but that the works of God should be made manifest in him. I must work the works of him that sent me, while it is day: the night cometh, when no man can work. As long as I am in the world I am the light of the world. When he had thus spoken, he spat on the ground, and made clay of the spittle, and he anointed the eyes of the blind man with the clay, And said unto him, Go, wash in the pool of Siloam (which is by interpretation, Sent.) He went his way therefore, and washed, and came seeing. The neighbours therefore, and they which before had seen him that he was blind, said, Is not this he that sat and begged? Some said, This is he: others said, He is like him: but he said, I am he. JOHN 9:1–9. *Related passages,* MATT. 9:27–30, 12:22, 20:30–34; MARK 10:46–52.

You can read a more extensive account in my books, *The Meaning Of Reincarnation,* and *Peace Within Yourself* which gives the psychological meaning of the book of *John.*

In ancient times it was believed that if a man were born blind, it was due to past *karma,* and that he was here to expiate for his sins. The people of that day also believed that the sins of the parents were communicated to the children. For example, if the parents were insane, all their children would be insane.

The *sin* spoken of in the Bible refers to the mental attitude, the mood, the feeling of the parents. All sin refers to movements of the mind rather than that of the body. Parents transmit their habitual thinking, fears, tensions, and false beliefs through the mind, not the body. Our feelings and moods create. What tone do you strike during the marital, creative act?

There are blind and deaf states of consciousness from which blind and deaf children come forth. Whatever tone is struck by the parents, a corresponding expression comes forth by the laws of reciprocal relationship.

There is no instance in the Bible in which anyone was ever refused a healing. The Absolute cannot and does not judge or condemn. All judgment is given to the son, *i.e.*, all judgment is pronounced in our own mind. Each man arrives at his own decision or conclusion, and there is an automatic response of the law. If man thinks negatively, the response is negative. If he thinks positively and constructively, the reaction of the law of his mind is good and very good.

The laws of nature and our mind cannot hold a grudge against us. There is not one law for a child and another for a man of ninety. The moment man goes within himself, claims his good, and presses his claim with faith and confidence, there is the automatic response of the law which honors the mental acceptance of his good. The past is forgotten and remembered no more.

Reason rejects the popular, superstitious belief of the people that man's blindness is due to his *karma*, that he may have blinded people in a former life and is now back on this plane to suffer and atone for his crime. Another very popular, superstitious belief was, and still is, that a child may be born blind because his parents were blind, or because they had sinned or had some physical disease. A man and wife though congenitally blind or blinded by accident may give birth to children with perfectly normal vision.

A mother through prayer, may change the mental and physical nature of her child while he is still in the womb, and bring about a perfect healing. In God's eyes there are no blind, deaf, halt, or lame people. God sees everyone perfect, and His Creation as Infinite Perfection.

I must work the works of him that sent me, while it is day. This means while the Light of Truth is shining, we consciously direct the law.

To make clay of the spittle represents a drooling state, like a boy hungers for candy and drools at the mouth. It represents a joyful, bubbling up state. You have seen geysers bubbling up which make clay look very much alive. The *clay* in the natural state represents the average man who is dead and unaware of the Healing Principle within him. He is, in other words, dead to his inner potentialities. As he awakens and becomes enthusiastic about the discovery of the powers within, he becomes alive to God; this is the meaning of *he spat on the ground and made clay of the spittle.* This latter phrase is an oriental, idiomatic, figurative expression meaning a deep, inner conviction that we now have the consciousness of what we want, and that we reject blindness or the old state of limitation.

We are not here to suffer or expiate for sins or errors. We are here to awaken to the Truth about ourselves and realize that *Beloved, now are we the sons of God*, that *Now is the day of salvation, and the Kingdom of Heaven is at hand.* Like Paul you can be changed in the twinkling of an eye.

Remember what is true of God is true of man. God can't possibly be blind, deaf, dumb, or sick. The Truth about man is that the Living Spirit Almighty is within him. God is all Bliss, Wholeness, Joy, Perfection, Harmony, and Peace. God is all the wonderful things you have ever heard of. There cannot possibly be any quarrel or division in this Boundless Wisdom. As you anchor your mind on these Eternal Verities about God, identify yourself with them mentally and a rearrangement of the thought patterns will take place in your mind and the Wholeness and Perfection of God will be made manifest.

The *clay* spoken of is a hard, dry, false belief. It is a muddy, confused mind which must be cleansed; then we *spit* (bring forth) our conviction of Truth.

Go wash in the pool of Siloam means give up and send away. Detach your consciousness from the old state which washes away the false idea and feel and affirm the spirituality of all substance. The blind state also represents our inability to see the state that would bless us. When man does not know that his savior is the realization of his heart's desire, he is truly blind.

We might also mention in this chapter dealing with the man born blind that all men are born blind. We are born into all that our environment represents. We have to learn how to choose and differentiate so that gradually we awaken to the Presence and Power of God within us.

There is a tendency among people to take everything literally. In your daily newspaper you may see a cartoon depicting some extravagance or waste in Government. You understand it as an allegorical picture of things, that is, visual allegory. We must remember that the Bible is an allegory in words. When people read of the blind, the halt, and the lame in the Bible they usually think of it only from the physical side.

We must see that there is also an internal deafness and an inner blindness though the eyes and ears may not be impaired or diseased in any way. A man can be psychologically lame when he is afraid to take on a new project. In some instances men refuse promotion because they are afraid they might fail. This is lameness even though the physical legs are perfect.

Dr. Nicoll of England stresses the fact that the transformation of meaning from the sensual or sensory level to the emotional and mental level is an act of faith.

For we walk by faith, not by sight: 2 COR. 5:7. Most people "walk by sight," that is, the literal meaning of everything dominates their consciousness. The blind man is the one who is blind inside.

In *Matthew* we read: *And, behold, two blind men sitting by the way side, when they heard that Jesus passed by, cried out, saying, Have mercy on us, O Lord, thou son of David. And the multitude rebuked them, because they should hold their peace: but they cried the more, saying, Have mercy on us, O Lord, thou son of David. And Jesus stood still, and called them, and said, What will ye that I shall do unto you? They say unto him, Lord, that our eyes may be opened. So Jesus had compassion on them, and touched their eyes: and immediately their eyes received sight, and they followed him.* MATT. 20:30–34.

The two blind men refers to the average man who walks the earth because he is intellectually and emotionally blind. We have a conscious and subconscious mind, *i.e.,* two phases or functions of the One Mind in all. If we do not consciously choose good thoughts and meditate on the lovely and beautiful, our intellect is blind. If we fail to realize and draw forth the wisdom, intelligence, and power of the subjective self, we are blind to the Kingdom of Heaven within.

A *blind man* thinks that hard work will make him wealthy. He fusses, frets, and fumes because he doesn't know that wealth is simply a state of consciousness. The feeling of wealth produces wealth; the feeling of health produces health. Confidence in the One Eternal Source and aligning ourselves mentally with it will take the form of wealth, health, peace, and all the blessed things of life.

I just spoke with a young actress who receives a thousand dollars a week for a few hours work each week. She said there were other actresses far prettier, more attractive, better educated than she, getting a hundred or a hundred and fifty dollars a week in small parts. Her explanation was that they had a low estimate of themselves and lacked confidence. They were blind and did not know that if we make a bargain with life for a penny a day, that is what we will receive. If they would overcome their estimate of themselves and claim their good in consciousness, there would be an automatic response, for *according to your belief is it done unto you.*

A few hours ago I chatted with a man who is leaving this city to take a sales manager job in San Francisco. Last month he was getting meager wages according to some union scale. *His eyes were opened* in our recent class on the inner meaning of the book of *Job.* He began to picture himself receiving congratulations from his wife on his marvelous promotion. He kept running the picture in his mind until it was fully developed in the subconscious, and much to his delight the promotion was confirmed objectively. The two blind states in him began to see because he brought about a harmonious union of his conscious and subconscious mind. These two phases synchronized and agreed on promotion, and what he subjectively felt as true became an objective manifestation.

The cry of the world is *Lord, that our eyes may be opened. Jesus* is your awareness of the Spiritual Power within you and your capacity to use it so that you can rise above any predicament or limitation.

The Bible says, *Jesus touched their eyes.* When you touch something you become aware of it as a sensation, a feeling. You have made contact, so to speak. You touch the Spiritual Power or the Presence of God with your thought, your mental picture.

And immediately their eyes received sight. This means that you will get an immediate response from the Spirit within you whose nature is responsiveness. You now receive your sight because you mentally perceive and lay hold of the Spiritual Power within you. You comprehend its nature and give it your sole allegiance and loyalty. The Maker of your eyes can heal your eyes.

Jesus is always *passing by* for the simple reason that your desire is your Jesus. Every problem has its solution or savior in the form of a desire. The desire is walking down the streets of your mind now. There is a *multitude* of fears, doubts, and anxious thoughts which challenges your desire and divides your allegiance. This is the multitude which, according to the parable, tries to restrain the blind men. *But they cried the more,* meaning that you must dynamically and decisively break through that motley crew of negative thoughts in your mind. You must push them all aside and have eyes only for your savior, *i.e.,* your desire.

Set your desire on high; love it; be loyal to it; kiss it affectionately; let it captivate you. You are now being loyal and you will succeed in touching the Healing Presence. At the moment you touch It, the Infinite Healing Power flows through the channel you created and your prayer is answered.

We should not ask for more Light. Rather, our prayer should be, "O God, give me eyes to see the Light." The Light of God always was, now is, and ever shall be. It is wonderful.

10

Walk with the Power of God

After this there was a feast of the Jews; and Jesus went up to Jerusalem. Now there is at Jerusalem by the sheep market a pool, which is called in the Hebrew tongue Bethesda, having five porches. In these lay a great multitude of impotent folk, of blind, halt, withered, waiting for the moving of the water. For an angel went down at a certain season into the pool, and troubled the water: whosoever then first after the troubling of the water stepped in was made whole of whatsoever disease he had. And a certain man was there, which had an infirmity thirty and eight years. When Jesus saw him lie, and knew that he had been now a long time in that case, he saith unto him, Wilt thou be made whole? The impotent man answered him, Sir, I have no man, when the water is troubled, to put me into the pool: but while

I am coming, another steppeth down before me. Jesus saith unto him, Rise, take up thy bed, and walk. John 5:1–8. *Related passages,* Luke 13:11–12.

Mankind is at the *pool.* The *pool* is consciousness, and all of us are living with our thoughts, feelings, beliefs, opinions, and mental images. Some of these states are *blind, halt, withered,* and *lame.* Furthermore, man is full of dreams, hopes, and aspirations which have never seen the light of day. Thousands are frustrated, unhappy, and sick because they have failed to realize their dreams, ideals, plans, and purposes. These dead hopes and dreams symbolize the *impotent folk, blind, halt, withered, waiting for the moving of the water.*

Are you waiting for something to happen? Don't sit around waiting for God to do something. You must begin, and when you begin Omnipotence begins to move on your behalf. God has provided you with everything. He has given you Himself; therefore, all His powers, qualities, and attributes are within you, waiting for you to call them forth and use them to grow.

Expand, unfold, and multiply your good a thousandfold. The initiative is with you. The God-Presence within is now governing all your vital organs, regulating your heart beat and general circulation. The earth, the stars, the sun, and moon, and the whole world is here for you to enjoy, but if you want to transcend your present concept of yourself, you must take the necessary steps.

Begin now to think constructively and heal the *blind, deaf,* and *withered* states within you. In this drama of healing, prayer is called a feast. When you meditate on your good, you are *feasting, i.e.,* you are consciously uniting with it; then you make it a living part of you in the same manner that a piece of bread becomes hair on your face or flesh of your body.

The pool has five porches which means we have five senses. Our senses usually deny what we pray for; furthermore, our five senses impregnate us with all kinds of rumors, false beliefs, and limitations.

Now you can put into application the teaching of this drama. You are *Jesus* when you recognize the Spiritual Power within as Omnipotent, and you enter *Jerusalem* (city of peace) when you still the mind and focus on the Living Spirit Almighty within you. You are now back at your Divine Center where you become perfectly quiet in God. You can enter into a deep peace, the Peace of God. You have exchanged the mood of worry and fear for the mood of faith, confidence, and an inner peace. This is why the Bible refers to a *sheep market.* All of us are in the market place every moment of our lives. You are constantly exchanging or giving up one idea for another. You must give up fear and buy faith in God and His Laws. Give up ill will and buy radiant good will. Give up the *blind states* in your belief and buy the idea that there is a way out of any problem. Contemplate the Truth that God has the answer, and therefore you know the answer.

The angel disturbs the pool. The *angel* spoken of is your desire, your wish. A man in our class on the "Miracles of Healing," on which this book is based, told me of a wrong done to him. He was very bitter. He had a desire for a Divine adjustment, but didn't know how to bring it about, and he was very disturbed. He learned how to resolve the conflict. *Whosoever stepped in first was made whole.* No one could get in before him. He was always in the Holy Omnipresence and he perceived the Truth that actually no one could really rob him or defraud him. When he learned of his Oneness with God and the fact that nothing can be lost, he realized his unity with the Infinite. He prayed that through the action of God his relationship with the other man was now transformed into order, harmony, goodness, and love. He began to see as God sees, and God sees everything in Infinite Perfection.

In other words, this young man ceased to gaze at the outward chaos and confusion, but he went within himself and claimed interior harmony and a Divine adjustment. The blurred, confused, outer picture was transformed into Divine order and peace between them. There was a remarkable solution. Trust the God-Wisdom which knows all and knows the way. "There's a Divinity that shapes our ends, Rough-hew them how we will."

In one of the class-lessons on the book of *Job*, which I have just finished, I told the students that if they had a problem, and could not see any way out, to sit still that night and quietly recognize the Presence of God within themselves, in the situation itself, and within all those concerned. After a few minutes of silent contemplation on that Truth, they were to turn the matter over completely to the subjective self, knowing it will order everything aright. This procedure kindles a fire in the heart which brings about an inner glow and warmth; and while this fire of love is burning in the heart, go off to sleep. Many received remarkable answers the next morning.

No one really can *get in before you*. No one can prevent you from realizing your goal or objective. The only power you are aware of is your own thought. When you think, that process is really Omnipotence in action. One with God is a majority. Your own thought causes the Omnipotent Power of God to move in your behalf. There is nothing to oppose, challenge, or thwart the action of the Infinite One. There can't be two omnipotent powers; if there were, one would cancel and neutralize the action of the other and there would be no order anywhere. There can't be two Infinites, that is unthinkable and mathematically impossible.

The Infinite moves, Troward tells you, as unity, as oneness, as wholeness, and as harmony. Your mind must also move as a unity, a sense of oneness with your ideal. If you are divided in your mind by acknowledging some other power, you are like a soldier marking time, you get nowhere and reach an impasse. Your mind is divided, two ideas or thoughts are quarreling. You must be the referee and come to a decision by realizing that there is but One Power; and that being so, you are free from fear. Desire without fear is realization.

Recall to mind that the suggestions of others, the race mind and its fears have no power over you. External conditions and suggestions of others are not causative. Your thought is in control. If you say that the other hurt you or made you angry, it means you permitted yourself to move in thought negatively. It was your fault and not the other person's. The other person is certainly not responsible for the way you think about him or the way you think in general. When you think of God, you are one with Omnipotence. The Source is Love; It knows no fear.

While I am coming, another steppeth down before me. Have you ever said that? Perhaps not, but you have heard people say, "It was John's fault," "Except for Mary or Johnny I would have been promoted." If you say anything of that nature, your allegiance is divided and you are disloyal to the One Power which knows no other. *I am God and there is no God beside me.*

I am sure that you are very familiar with the fact that no one can say *I AM* for you. That statement is in the first person, present tense. It means you are announcing the Presence of God within as Cause and Creator. Notice when you speak to your sister or son you say, "You are." When you speak in the third person you say, "They are."

One of our students in the Bible class on the book of *John** said to herself, "I possess the power to say "I AM." No one can say it for me. I now believe I AM what I wish to be. I live, move, and have my being in that mental atmosphere and no person, place, or thing can get in before me or prevent me from being what I long to be; for, *according to my belief, is it done unto me.*" She had a remarkable demonstration using the above prayer.

The *impotent man* is the man who does not know where the power is and believes it is outside himself. The *thirty and eight years* in the numerical symbology or science of the Bible means the conviction of God's

---

* See Chapter 5 in my book *Peace Within Yourself.*

Presence and coming of age spiritually. The number *thirty* refers to the Trinity or the creative working of our own mind; the *eight* means the octave or man's capacity to rise higher through knowledge of mental and spiritual laws. The Trinity is your thought and feeling and from the fusion of these comes the third step which is the conviction of your good, or God. When your idea is mothered by feeling or emotion and the two become one, you are at peace, and God is Peace. You are constantly putting the Trinity into operation. Ouspensky used to call the third element which entered in the neutral element. We call it God.

The idea of perfect health can be resurrected by you as you now claim, feel, and believe that the Healing Principle is instantly transforming your whole being into God's Perfect Pattern of harmony, health, and peace.

I read a remarkable article which appeared in the magazine *Nautilus* some years ago. It was written by Frederick Elias Andrews of Indianapolis. He said that as a boy he was pronounced incurable. He began to pray and from a crooked, twisted, cripple going about on hands and knees, he became a strong, straight, well-formed man. This young man decided what he wanted and that was a perfect healing. He created his own affirmation, mentally absorbing the qualities he needed. He affirmed over and over again: "I am whole, perfect, strong, powerful, loving, harmonious, and happy." He persevered and said that this prayer was the last thing on his lips at night and the first thing in the morning. He prayed for others also by sending out thoughts of love and health. This attitude of mind and way of prayer returned to him multiplied. Like Job of old who prayed for his friends, God gave him twice as much as he had before. His faith and perseverance paid off big dividends. Negative thoughts came to him but he did not entertain them. When thoughts of anger, jealousy, fear, or worry came into his mind, he would start his affirmation going in his mind. The answer to all fearful thoughts is to turn on the lamp of love forever burning in your heart.

The man in the Bible had the infirmity *thirty and eight years.* We have already discussed the Trinity. The number *eight* is added when healing takes place. *Eight* is composed of two circles representing the synchronous or harmonious interaction of your conscious and subconscious mind, or idea and feeling. When your desire and your emotional nature agree, there is no longer any quarrel between the two, and a healing follows.

The command by Jesus, or your own illumined reason, *Rise, take up thy bed and walk,* is your voice of authority, based on your inner conviction telling you that you are healed. We can actually hear the inner sound of our belief. It is veritably a command on the inside. You have *taken up your bed* (truth) and walk the earth a free man. All this happens on the *sabbath*.

The *sabbath* is an inner certitude or inner stillness which follows true prayer. It is really a state of mind in which you are unconcerned, unmoved, and undisturbed, because you know that just as surely as the sun rises in the morning there will be a resurrection of your desire. When you have reached the point of complete mental acceptance, you are resting in the sabbath or in the conviction "It is done." *And it was on the sabbath day he was healed.*

11

The Impossible Made Possible

I shall give the highlights of the wonderful healing technique in the raising of Lazarus mentioned in Chapter Eleven of *John*. For a complete, detailed interpretation of this wonderful chapter, I recommend my book *Peace Within Yourself*, which is an interpretation, chapter by chapter, of the book of *John*.

Lazarus represents any dead state, the desire, plan, enterprise, or goal which is frozen within and has not been made alive and resurrected in your world of experience. It may also represent your desire for health which has failed to materialize.

Jesus at the grave of Lazarus represents you and your awareness of the Power which can resurrect your ideal which has been covered with the *grave clothes* of fear, doubt, and anxiety for a long time, and has been *suppressed in the tomb* of the subconscious.

Jesus said, Take ye away the stone. The stone of superstition, fear, and ignorance must be removed. *Martha*, representing the worldly viewpoint says to you, *"By this time he stinketh: for he hath been dead four days." Four* represents the completed state, the termination, the manifestation. According to sense-evidence the situation seems absolutely hopeless, or the condition may seem to be incurable. Regardless of the external circumstances, even though the whole world would deny what you pray for, *if thou wouldest believe, thou shouldest see the glory of God.*

In other words, if you will turn away from sense-evidence and go within and contemplate the reality of what you pray for, and sing the song of triumph, you will see the Glory of God—you will see the answer to your prayer. *To believe* is to live in the state of being or having what you pray for. Your thought is your belief, and whatever you think, you become. Live with the thought and reality of the answered prayer, and there will be an atomic and molecular change in the diseased body to conform to the new mental pattern.

The stone is lifted as you positively refuse to give power to sickness, disease, or fear. As you give all power to God, *the stone is removed* and you are no longer weighted down with the burdens of the world.

Your new mental attitude is *the angel who rolls away the stone of* fear and false belief.

You are now *Jesus, lifting up your eyes saying, Father, I thank thee that thou hast heard me. And I knew that thou hearest me always. He cried with a loud voice, Lazarus, come forth.* JOHN 11:41–43. These latter verses give a magnificent formula for prayer. The thankful attitude works miracles.

Many years ago, a friend of mine who had tuberculosis took these wonderful words of the Bible, *I thank thee Father that thou hast heard me, and I knew that thou hearest me always.* He reasoned it out this way. His human father always gave him whatever he promised him. At one time his father promised him a trip to France (he lived in Ireland). The trip was to take place in August, but the promise was made in May. He remembered how joyous and enthusiastic he was. He recalled bubbling over with expectancy and being thrilled beyond words. This happened even though the trip had not taken place. All he had was the promise; he knew it was certain because his father never failed him.

He said to himself, "Why shouldn't I be thankful and grateful to my Heavenly Father for the promise of perfect health, for 'I know that he heareth me always,' 'I will restore health unto thee and I will heal thee of thy wounds saith the Lord.'" Two or three times a day he would still his mind, relax, and let go. Then he would imagine he was talking to the Invisible Healing Presence within, and he began to whisper, "Thank you," over and over again. He did this until his mind was saturated with the feeling of thankfulness. At the end of three weeks the sputum test and all the others were completely negative. He cast God's Spell over himself. He became magnetized as he contemplated the harmony and perfection of God which he knew would be experienced by him, as it was already given to him by God. When he contemplated the Peace, Order, and Healing Power of God within him, there was a complete rearrangement of the atoms of his body. He became like a magnetized piece of steel which draws to itself other steel, and not nickel and other metals. In the diseased state he was demagnetized, the atoms were still present, but he ceased to vibrate harmony, health, and peace. His feeling of thankfulness and sense of confidence in the One Healing Power drew like a magnet the conviction that made him healthy, vital, harmonious, and whole.

Like the man mentioned above, give up the false belief that other powers can make you ill without your consent. Contemplate yourself the way you want to be, happy, healthy, radiant, and strong. Identify yourself with these qualities, and accept nothing else. Give up completely all fear in any other so-called causes or powers. Reject categorically and dynamically all false beliefs. Turn in confidence to the Supreme Power within which moves as your feeling, your faith, and trust. When you do this, you are becoming a marvelous mental and spiritual magnet and you will inevitably attract harmony, health, peace, and joy.

The three steps in *raising Lazarus from the dead are:*

1. Recognition of your consciousness as supreme cause.
2. Accept the idea of perfect health and live with it in your mind. To believe is to live with the idea, *i.e.,* make it alive.
3. The inevitable conviction which follows the previous two steps. You are now filled with the feeling of being what you want to be.

Your mood is now one of authority and you say inwardly, *Lazarus, come forth.*

This is the command from the inside of the one who knows that *I and my Father are one.*

12

A Prayer for Healing

A personal healing will ever be the most convincing evidence of the power of prayer. About thirty-five years ago I resolved a malignancy by using a prayer based on the 139th Psalm. I had just heard an interpretation of the Psalm and was meditating intensely on its profundity.

For thou hast possessed my reins: thou hast covered me in my mother's womb. I will praise thee; for I am fearfully and wonderfully made: marvellous are thy works; and that my soul knoweth right well. My substance was not hid from thee, when I was made in secret, and curiously wrought in the lowest parts of the earth. Thine eyes did see my substance, yet being imperfect; and in thy book all my members were written, which in continuance were fashioned, when as yet there was none of them.

This magnificent, inspired Psalm teaches that the body and its organs are formed in idea before it is made manifest, just as surely as we can observe that a watchmaker has the idea first in mind before the watch becomes an objective reality. Creative Intelligence fashions and molds the entire body. The Intelligence that creates the body must know how to heal it; furthermore, the Psalm states that *in thy book all my members were written.* The *book* is the Life Principle where the archetype of all organs are inscribed.

Using this Psalm as a basis for my prayer, I prayed in a very simple way as follows:

"My body was made in secret by God. His Wisdom fashioned all my organs, tissues, muscles, and bones. His Healing Power saturates my mind and body, making we whole and perfect. I will give thanks unto thee. Wonderful are thy works."

I prayed aloud for about five minutes two or three times a day, repeating this simple prayer. In about three months my skin was whole and perfect.

Wonderful are thy works; and that my soul knoweth right well.

About the Author

A native of Ireland who resettled in America, Joseph Murphy, Ph.D., D.D. (1898–1981) was a prolific and widely admired New Thought minister and writer, best known for his metaphysical classic, *The Power of Your Subconscious Mind*, an international bestseller since it first appeared on the self-help scene in 1963. A popular speaker, Murphy lectured on both American coasts and in Europe, Asia, and South Africa. His many books and pamphlets on the auto-suggestive and metaphysical faculties of the human mind have entered multiple editions—some of the most poignant of which appear in this volume. Murphy is considered one of the pioneering voices of affirmative-thinking philosophy.

Printed in the USA
CPSIA information can be obtained
at www.ICGtesting.com
JSHW01203614082 4
68134JS00033B/3084